PREACHING
FROM THE GRAVE

PREACHING
FROM THE GRAVE

A Story of Faith From the
Rwanda Genocide

PHODIDAS NDAMYUMUGABE, PHD

Pacific Press®
Publishing Association
Nampa, Idaho | www.pacificpress.com

Cover design by Gerald Lee Monks
Cover illustration from iStockphoto.com
Cover photo provided by the author
Inside design by Aaron Troia

The author assumes full responsibility for the accuracy of all facts and quotations as cited in this book.

Scripture quotations marked NIV are from THE HOLY BIBLE, NEW INTERNATIONAL VERSION®. Copyright © 1973, 1978, 1984, 2011 by Biblica, Inc.® Used by permission. All rights reserved worldwide.

Scripture quotations marked NKJV are taken from the New King James Version®. Copyright © 1982 by Thomas Nelson. Used by permission. All rights reserved.

You can obtain additional copies of this book by calling toll-free 1-800-765-6955 or by visiting www.AdventistBookCenter.com.

Library of Congress Cataloging-in-Publication Data

Names: Ndamyumugabe, Phodidas, 1970- author.
Title: Preaching from the grave : the amazing story of how God saved a young man's life on
   multiple occasions during the Rwandan genocide and used him to witness to killers /
   Phodidas Ndamyumugabe, Ph.D.
Description: Nampa : Pacific Press Publishing Association, 2019. | Summary: "Stories from the
   Rwandan genocide and how they affected the mission work"—Provided by publisher.
Identifiers: LCCN 2019024758 | ISBN 9780816365814 (paperback) | ISBN9780816365821
   (kindle edition)
Subjects: LCSH: Ndamyumugabe, Phodidas, 1970- | Christian biography—Rwanda.
   | Missions—Rwanda. | Rwanda—History—Civil War, 1994. | Genocide—Rwanda.
Classification: LCC BR1725.N345 A3 2019 | DDC 276.7571/082092 [B]—dc23
LC record available at https://lccn.loc.gov/2019024758

July 2019

Dedication

This book is dedicated to my wife, Jacqueline Basime; my sons, Paulin, Pedro, and Pagiel; and all who love God and want to live a faithful life until our Lord Jesus Christ returns!

Contents

Preface

This book is the personal story of Dr. Phodidas Ndamyumugabe's experience during and around the 1994 genocide against Tutsis in Rwanda. Parts of the story have appeared and been distributed in different documents. Some of the story was distributed worldwide through the quarterly mission stories of the Seventh-day Adventist Church as well as in a coauthored book, *Rwanda, Beyond Wildest Imagination*.

Preaching From the Grave is a more comprehensive version of his story. It relates how God miraculously intervened in his life and answered prayers on multiple occasions. Dr. Ndamyumugabe wrote the story with the intention of helping readers know that the God of Daniel, Shadrach, Meshach, and Abednego still deals with His children today in the same way He dealt with those faithful men so long ago!

It is the author's hope that readers will understand that when one remains "faithful until death" (Revelation 2:10, NKJV), God can still work miracles, just as He did for His people in the past—even if one has more than just one foot in the grave!

Acknowledgments

Friends motivated me to write this story because they felt it would encourage and strengthen the faith of believers around the world. Many people have contributed in different ways to this book's completion. I would like to thank Dr. Zvandasara Nkoziyabo, who motivated me to write and agreed to co-author the first version of my testimony. My special thanks go to Dr. Verlyn Benson and Anita Benson for their encouragement and support, which I needed to produce this story.

I also want to thank Donald Macintosh, my pastor at Weimar Seventh-day Adventist Church, for moral support and help in various ways. I would like to express my gratitude to other friends at Weimar Institute and elsewhere who contributed in different ways. They have provided moral encouragement, read and introduced the book, and assisted in the editing and design of the book. In a special way, recognition goes to Trina Feliciano who, with untiring effort, spent quality and quantity time in editing the manuscript.

I wish to thank those Rwandans who demonstrated their belief that all human beings deserve love, because God created them in His image. This includes those soldiers of the RPA and some Hutus who sacrificed all in trying to save human lives. These became instruments in the hands of God as they labored to rescue victims from the clutches of the killers and strove to restore peace and unity among Rwandans.

I could not forget to thank those leaders in Rwanda who, for the last two decades, have worked hard to restore and maintain peace. They have encouraged unity, reconciliation, and love among the people of Rwanda. Government and religious leaders have done the almost impossible work of bringing together all Rwandans as one people, despite what had happened in the country.

Finally, I say, to God be the glory for the things He has done! Had the

Preaching From the Grave

Lord not been there when men sought to end my life, I would be resting in the grave. But praise be to the name of the Lord who allowed me to come out of my grave, live more years, and write this story about His unchanging promises. My help is in the name of the Lord, the Maker of heaven and earth (see Psalm 124).

Introduction

This book is a must read of how God protected His own during one of the most widespread slaughters of all time. Amid a genocide initiated by the worst of evil passions, and propelled by deception, misplaced fear, and brute force, one man refused to deceive others to save his life and remained transparent in his worship of the true God and honored Him by keeping all of His commandments through the most extreme circumstances. This story is no less compelling than the story of Shadrach, Meshach, and Abednego. No logical objective mind can come away from either story believing there is no God. The difference in this story is the repeated "fiery furnace" miracles hour after hour and day after day. Evil had set up deadly trap after trap and multiple back-up traps to be sure of accomplishing its intent. But even the most well-laid plans crafted by the devil himself will fail when God intervenes to protect those that are truly His. Dr. Phodidas's life is an example to us all and especially to young people. As you read this story, you will learn how you might maintain emotional calm under the most severe physical, mental, emotional, social, and spiritual attacks that can be imagined. How proud I am that Dr. Phodidas is rightly training an army of youth to stand up for God with truth and love at Weimar Institute today.

—Neil Nedley, MD, president, Weimar Institute

In 2016, my wife and I accepted an assignment in Rwanda, Africa. During the subsequent months and years that followed, we were frequently reminded of the atrocities that occurred during the Rwandan Genocide. During our first year of work, 675 students completed their education. Finances were tight, and it became necessary to raise tuition *and* find at least 675 new students to replace those who had graduated. Dr. Phodidas, our theology professor, came to my office and volunteered to help recruit students. During that summer, he brought nearly one thousand new students to the university for admission. Meanwhile, for camp meetings, speaking engagements, or for just a sermon or chapel talk, Dr. Phodidas became my trusted translator. Little by little I learned more about his personal life. Enclosed in the chapters of this book is an incredible story of survival during numerous vicious manhunts. It is a thrilling story of God's care and intervention that you will never forget!

—Dr. Verlyn R. Benson, VPAA Weimar Institute

The stories and message of this book changed my life. It is not theoretic, having been written by one who has experienced a literal time of trouble. Each story builds on the last, in a way that will reveal not only the riveting story but also the condition of your own heart. As I read and was able to listen to the testimony of Dr. Phodidas, I realized that his story reveals what is necessary if one is to remain faithful in times of trouble. May God convict your heart as you read, and may we each be prepared to face the conflicts of this life with the courage and character that only Christ can give.

—Don Mackintosh, senior church pastor
and head of the Department of Theology, Weimar Institute

1

Fond Memories of My Childhood

Listen, my sons, to a father's instruction;
pay attention and gain understanding.
I give you sound learning,
so do not forsake my teaching.
For I too was a son to my father,
still tender, and cherished by my mother.
Then he taught me, and he said to me,
"Take hold of my words with all your heart;
keep my commands, and you will live.
Get wisdom, get understanding;
do not forget my words or turn away from them.
Do not forsake wisdom, and she will protect you;
love her, and she will watch over you."

—Proverbs 4:1–6

I was born on October 3, 1970, in Kibuye,* a province about 130 kilometers (80 miles) west of Kigali, the capital of Rwanda. I was the final addition to a family of eight children. Growing up, one of my sweetest memories was of being pampered, an experience many last-born children hold in common. I was the center of my parents' love, and my siblings affectionately used many nicknames to describe their love for me or the values they wanted me to develop. I grew up feeling loved but also challenged to live up to my family's expectations.

---

* Today, the name Kibuye as a province has changed and it is called Karongi.

Preaching From the Grave

In our part of the country, life was tough. We learned to work at a very early age. By the time I was nine, I was in charge of caring for our family's animals. I did not enjoy being placed in charge of the cows, especially when the weather turned cold. Splitting the towering trees for firewood was another of my duties.

For me, one of the most challenging times was waking up every morning, rain or shine, to lead our animals to pasture where they would feed for the day. My parents trained us to work hard in all circumstances, no matter how we felt. Laziness was not permitted. Even at lunchtime my niece and I were expected to do some chore as a family assignment before returning to class.

The discipline I went through at this young age had nothing to do with our financial status. No one had much money in this rural area, but we had the minimum needed for our well-being. Though we had house-helpers who could have done most of the work without my contribution, my parents expected me to assist with the daily duties. Work was the principle of life, and everyone had to be involved if they hoped to live independently in the future.

Despite the difficulties of living in a rural area of western Rwanda, our mountain life held many advantages that far outweighed the more luxurious life in the cities. Some of those benefits I can understand only now that I am old enough to miss them, yet others I could understand and appreciate even while I was still a young boy.

My family lived in a place where you could hardly look three hundred feet without seeing another hill. Hills are characteristic of Rwanda, which is commonly known as "the country of a thousand hills." But Kibuye is unique, because there are also mountains, some of which are the tallest in the country. These mountains make the weather always pleasant, never too warm or too cold.

The most scenic feature in this part of the world is probably Kivu Lake. It is a beautiful body of water dotted with small conical-shaped islands from which one may jump into the clear waters below. These islands caught my attention as a child. As a young boy, I enjoyed seeing their shadows reflected on the waters, creating varied colors and beauty as the sun rose and set.

Growing up, we didn't need swimming pools, because the clear lake waters, cradled by solid white volcanic rock, were ideal. Volcanic insulation

Fond Memories of My Childhood

kept the waters at a consistent temperature of about twenty-four degrees Celsius (seventy-five degrees Fahrenheit). This made the lake a good source of recreation and refreshment, whatever the weather. Whenever it was cool outside, the lake felt warm, and when it became warmer outside, the water stayed cool.

This beautiful lake was central to many of my childhood memories. I remember keeping animals around the lake and diving with friends to chase the fish in the depths of its waters. I recall running bare-chested as a child into the cool waters to refresh myself during the noon heat.

But even greater than my appreciation for the geographical features of my home village, I knew my family life was the most important blessing for me. Since I was the last-born in my large family of eight children, many of my nieces and nephews were around my age or even slightly older. This gave me the opportunity to have many friends who were also family members.

Every single vacation, I visited my siblings' homes just to enjoy the company of my nieces and nephews. Life was sweet at this tender age. Every vacation time was a celebration. I made it a habit to spend time with my siblings after finishing the duties assigned by my mother—sometimes at their homes, sometimes at my own. Every time we visited, we would always stay up outside the house at night, basking either in the full moonlight or under a starlit sky.

We often exchanged African stories which our parents had told us to teach us cultural and biblical values. We liked to compete in our storytelling, taking turns one after the other. Life was blissful, and love was the undeniable theme in our home.

However, as I grew up, though content with family love, I could sense a need for improvement in our environment. My family was relatively comfortable in terms of material possessions. My parents could supply our family's needs, and we had no shortage of food or clothing. But living standards in Kibuye were so low that it was difficult for ordinary people to buy even a bike. We were satisfied with our humble way of life, but as I grew older and visited the neighboring cities, I saw a different way of living. I soon felt the need to take my family to a higher level.

In this spirit and out of love for my family, I determined to study diligently and work hard so that one day I could make a change in the lives of my family members. Like most kids, I remember often talking about my dreams and promising my mother that one day I would provide for our family's needs and give her a happier life.

My mother had a caring nature, but she also dealt strictly with me. She was so strict that during my childhood I often felt her rules were too heavy. As I grew up, however, I understood that she was the best mother I could ever have wished for in life.

When guests were visiting our family or my sisters had come back home, which happened often, she would talk about the love she had for me and what a good boy I was. I knew she always had something positive to say about me, and I felt great about this.

However, her facial expression inspired fear whenever I knew I had done something displeasing or contrary to the family order. Looking into her eyes in those moments, I learned the difference between good and evil, virtue and vice. The consequences of not doing what was right gave me a picture of how God hates sin. In the same way, her public joy and her compliments for me when I did right taught me how God considers us when we are behaving according to His will.

Like other mothers, she did her job of educating in the home. My mother longed to see my future, and I often heard her say so. She looked forward to seeing me finish my studies, becoming the man she had envisioned as she disciplined, encouraged, and coached me in all areas of life. Unfortunately, as sometimes happens in this life, she did not live long enough to see the fruits of her work. She passed away before I finished high school due to an untreated stomach illness, probably undiagnosed cancer.

The lessons I learned from my family helped me feel a deep love for God at a young age and to recognize the importance of obedience. I remember giving my life to Jesus in the third year of my elementary education when I was nine years old. Our church was close to my home, which gave me opportunities to attend every worship service. I was always sitting in the first pew, and every time there was an altar call, I eagerly responded to the pastor's invitation to make a commitment to God.

Church made a meaningful difference in my life. I enjoyed every worship service, and each sermon left a tremendous impact on my mind during those early years. I still remember specific pastors as well as their sermons and illustrations.

Some of the most touching moments in my spiritual life as a child were

Fond Memories of My Childhood

the times for prayer. Our church had drums, which in those days were used to remind church members that the hour for prayer had come. There were church members who knew how to make drums, and each church usually had five or six of them ready for use. The beat of drums echoing in the mountains preceded every worship service, beckoning us to congregate for worship.

Weeks of Prayer were some of the most important times we had. Since I lived near the church, I was often up earlier than anyone else, sometimes starting to beat the drum several hours before sunrise. I did this to wake up everyone in the village so they would come to the church, which was the center of spiritual and social life for Seventh-day Adventists. Sometimes we would play the drums for hours. The playing had nothing to do with dancing, but the combination of rhythms was so beautiful and attracted both youth and adults for worship.

Everything was about to change, but one thing would remain to mark my past heritage and determine my future spiritual life. Among my seven siblings, was a sister who seemed to love God more than all the others. She had read the Bible from cover to cover in her youth and had underlined all her favorite verses. When she was married, she distributed gifts to all our family members. Everyone received gifts, and since I perceived she loved me the most, I thought I would surely deserve a gift. When she appeared to have given out every gift, I wondered what she would give me! I felt somewhat angry with her, because it seemed she had forgotten me.

I thought there were no more material things she could give me, but in reality, she had kept back a surprise. One morning, she approached me and said the gift she had set aside for me was a Bible. This was not a new Bible; it was her old Bible, filled with underlined verses and promises. Since I did not have a Bible of my own, I accepted it with some resentment. This was not what I had expected! It certainly was a surprise. It wasn't until later that I realized it was one of the best gifts I could have ever received.

From that time on, whenever I was not at school, I was reading my Bible. I didn't know what this would do for me until years later. At this point in my life, I read it as if it were an assignment.

As I read that Bible through, the part that attracted me the most was the book of Proverbs. I remember reading in this book what wisdom is all about. Every time I read passages and stories from the Bible, I felt as if they were speaking directly to me. The story of Elijah's faithfulness affected me greatly.

Preaching From the Grave

I often prayed that God would help me be as wise as He wanted me to be and that I would be able to stand firm like Elijah on Mount Carmel.

2

Prepared for the Crisis

*"For the eyes of the L*ORD *run to and fro throughout the whole earth, to show Himself strong on behalf of those whose heart is loyal to Him."*
—2 Chronicles 16:9, NKJV

When something terrible is about to happen, God will alert His people. He helps them know what may befall them and leads them through the needed preparation which allows them to stand firm in evil days. This preparation does not always happen positively, or at least not in the way one might desire. Sometimes God takes one through trying circumstances to prepare them for more challenging ones. When the time comes, one manages to stand firm amid a terrible crisis, as a trained soldier, having been conditioned to walk with God.

After finishing my primary education, I could not continue my studies in Rwanda. The government used a quota system to determine who could go on to high school. The regional and ethnic groups one belonged to would affect the chances of getting in. Many qualified young people had to end their pursuit of higher education because of this.

I knew it would not be easy for me to go to high school. The government ran most of the schools. Social and ethnic discrimination were common practices. My sister, who had given me her Bible before her marriage, was living in Goma, in the Democratic Republic of the Congo (previously called Zaire). I went to visit her, hoping I might gain access to a high school education there.

Knowing it was difficult for me to continue my education in Rwanda, my sister invited me to enroll in school in Goma as soon as I arrived. I gladly accepted her offer and soon started my studies at Mikeno High School. It did not take long, however, for me to feel life there would be too difficult.

Preaching From the Grave

Everything differed totally from my home. The food was not like the food I normally ate. The people were also different. From the government officials to the jobless peasants on the street, it seemed that most of them were unethical. Many didn't even try to hide their corrupt practices.

Soon after I started my studies, my peers elected me to be the class captain. My first disappointment came when the teacher asked me to collect money from students. He expected them to pay him for their grades. According to him, one had to pay a certain amount of money for a certain level of grades. There was no reason to write exams or tests correctly. What mattered was to have the amount of money needed for the grade one wanted to have in each test or exam. Because of my Christian beliefs, I resolved not to defile myself with this evil practice. This made my teacher furious, and he notified me that I would not pass.

It wasn't long before I felt the effects of my determined decision. I had consistently scored the highest in daily quizzes and assignments and felt confident I would have the best final result. The teacher, however, rated me third in my class, with an almost failing grade of 60 percent. To my astonishment, the top student probably should have been one of the lowest-scoring among about forty in the class.

I soon realized that the students were as corrupt as the teachers. As the class captain, I was the one who called attendance; it was my duty to indicate who was present or absent. Some students expected me to mark them present when they were absent.

Because their negotiations did not work with me, they soon became my enemies. I was not paid for being class captain, so I thought it would be easy to give it up and no longer have the responsibility, thus avoiding conflicts and the retaliation of my disgruntled teacher and peers. But there was no chance of this happening. The school administration would not allow me to do this and demanded that I continue on as class captain.

It seemed there was no way out. The teachers were corrupt, and the students wanted me to be corrupt as well. I realized I was now alone; I had no one to share my plight with. I decided to pray that God would help me. This was the first time I felt the need to pray for God to help me through a disastrous situation. Several times I faced bad boys who wanted me to change their attendance status. Since I was unwilling to cooperate, they would insult me in class and threaten that gangs would beat me up.

Prepared for the Crisis

I resolved that I would not dishonor my God regardless of what might happen. Instead, I chose to intensify my prayers, asking God to help me get through the school year. Every time there was a problem, I'd open the door of the classroom, go inside, and say a prayer. I also prayed before each exam and asked God to be in control.

As a result of my prayers, my colleagues and the teachers finally realized I was not going to give in, and they left me alone. After this, I enjoyed the rest of the school year without a problem. Also, the Lord encouraged my zeal for Him. On the day when the yearly results were announced, I was not only the top of my class but also the top of the whole school of hundreds of students.

The school principal called me before the entire assembly and had me stand before them. After announcing my grade, he challenged everyone to work the following year as I had. At the end of that next year, I was again the top student. I realized that God is always on the side of the oppressed, especially when it is for the sake of His name.

I completed the following two years of my high school education—but with challenges. The reason had nothing to do with the external problems I faced, but with the compromises I made. Because of my exceptional school performance, I was admitted to an elite school, and my new environment somehow blinded me. I was in what some would call the best high school in the region, privileged to be among the few young people who could attend this school. Most of my teachers were Europeans. I was excited about the new knowledge I would attain and the possibility of a better future.

Somehow, this made me forget about my principles regarding Sabbath keeping. I was a Seventh-day Adventist, and I knew I was supposed to rest on the Sabbath. The school I was now attending was a Roman Catholic institution. Classes were held every day of the week except Sunday.

Failing to uphold my standards for a while made me understand the dangers of a new environment. The new friends we make, a new job, or a new school can challenge our spiritual principles. These things can prove to be a benefit or, if one is not careful, they can sometimes thwart one's goals and best purposes in life. We often underestimate their potential to blind our minds and divert us from our spiritual path.

Soon, my excitement at attending this new school turned into confusion and doubt. I was now wondering whether or not to study on the Sabbath. Unfortunately, it took some time before I made my final decision. While trying to convince myself that there was no other option but to disregard the Sabbath by going ahead with my studies, God gave me a message that made it clear what was happening. This helped convince me that if I was going to be faithful to God, I had to stop going to school on the Sabbath, even at the expense of facing dismissal from the school.

During the time I was studying on Sabbath, I attended every Sabbath afternoon program at the Seventh-day Adventist church in Goma. A church elder, Mr. Kabwe, was teaching from the book of Revelation. I attended every meeting and determined not to miss a single lecture. As I went through the study, I got a better understanding of what is going on with this world. Every lecture convinced me more that Jesus is in control of all that happens in this life.

Jesus holding the seven stars and walking among the seven candlesticks (Revelation 1:9–20) really captured my attention. Also, subjects like the seven churches (Revelation 2; 3) and the seven seals (Revelation 6; 8:1) became of interest as I came to discover that these prophecies were about the revelation of Jesus to His people (Revelation 1:1–3) and not just mysteries, unknowable to humans.

Week after week, I studied the prophecies. The more I studied, the more I became convinced that the details in the seven churches and the seven seals in the book of Revelation are describing the situation of the church throughout the ages. I came to believe that these images say the same thing in different ways and that they all were designed to prove to the church that Jesus is in control and knows what is going on until the end. As I understood them, these prophecies, in their respective order, were to serve as a roadmap, leading the church to the day of Jesus' second coming.

I became convinced that we are living in the last moments of the history of humanity and that what God requires is faithfulness from His followers— keeping His commandments and having the faith of Jesus (Revelation 12:17; 14:12). I resolved that I must do whatever God wanted me to do at any cost. My love for Him was intensifying in a way that could be experienced only by someone who learns the Bible earnestly and prayerfully.

The decision I made was not as easy as I thought it would be. This was a school which I believed would allow me to succeed in life and go back to my home village as somebody who could provide for the needs of my family. Stopping my studies would mean failure. I felt conflicted inside. One Friday evening, I struggled with whether I should go to school or to church the next morning.

I remember praying and asking God to work a miracle for me so I would know what decision to make. I told Him that if it was a sin to go to school on the Sabbath, He needed to make me unable to move when I woke up. To my way of thinking, this would convince me of God's will for me concerning the Sabbath. I know now that this was a faulty prayer. God had taught me what is right, and I needed to follow His revealed will without question. But when I woke up the next morning, I could move. I believed I had God's approval to continue my daily studies, so I went to school again on Sabbath.

The following Sabbath, however, I decided to obey God, regardless of the consequences. I knew the principal, who was a Roman Catholic priest, would not understand my motive for not studying on Saturdays. The school policies were very strict and unbending. Also, even if the principal didn't dismiss me from the school, there seemed to be no way I would pass my classes without studying every day.

As soon as I started going to church each Sabbath, my absences at school became obvious. I missed several exams and tests given on Saturdays, and teachers realized I was absent from all their Saturday classes.

They reported the matter to the principal, who soon invited me to meet with him to offer an explanation. As I tried to answer his questions, he seemed not to have any arguments to present to me. Instead, he seriously cautioned me and handed me a letter which he had prepared ahead of time. The letter offered two options: I could attend the school every day except Sunday and comply with the school administration, or I could leave the school and join a Seventh-day Adventist school that supported my religious convictions.

It was a Monday morning when I reported to the principal's office. I had about four more days to ponder my decision and determine what I would do. That week was painful. I kept thinking of how I might return to my village without finishing my education. But I had made my final decision.

During the week, I contacted local Adventist leaders and asked them to intervene on my behalf. Before Sabbath arrived, I had to make sure I had secured authorization from the school administration to allow me to continue my studies while still holding fast to my religious convictions. On Friday, the president of my church's local mission field and the mission treasurer visited my school and met with the principal to discuss my case.

Preaching From the Grave

After their departure, the principal called me into his office to warn me again. He informed me about the visit from my church representatives, and he reiterated that his decision was the same. Nothing they said had changed his mind. I needed to abide by the school rules or leave and find another school with different rules.

When the Sabbath came, there was but one option for me—simple obedience to God's Word and leaving the consequences in His hands. I headed to church as planned. It was a walking distance of about three kilometers (two miles) from my home.

On my way to church that morning, something troubled my mind for a while. I saw a group of young people whose parents I well knew were Adventists. One girl was the daughter of a church pastor. As I watched them walking to school with their books, disturbing thoughts came to my mind. Could it be that I had been misled in believing theories taught by pastors? Did these people, including the pastor, realize that we must observe the Sabbath and that eternal life involves faithfulness to God (see Revelation 2:10)?

As I pondered the course I was taking and wondered if I might be mistaken, I sensed that one does not win the spiritual battle by a simple knowledge of biblical truth. I reasoned that faithfulness has nothing to do with church leadership. If that were the case, the Sadducees during the time of Jesus would have accepted Him. I felt comforted by God's Spirit bringing these things to my mind as I continued on my way to church.

Two things happened when I arrived at school the following Monday morning. First, the principal had been informed that I did not come to school on Saturday, and he had decided to chase me away from the school. Second, my church leaders, having tried in vain to convince the principal, had appealed to the bishop of the regional Roman Catholic Church. The bishop had given a letter to my church president informing the principal of my right to attend the Roman Catholic school while following my religious convictions!

That Monday, as soon as I entered the principal's office, I handed over the letter from the bishop. After reading it through, he looked at me with penetrating eyes and said, "You have disobeyed me, your leader. I will also disobey my leader, just as you have disobeyed me, and dismiss you from this school." From his perspective, my behavior showed disobedience to him, while for me, it was a matter of faithfulness to God.

Prepared for the Crisis

After trying my best to convince him that it wasn't about me disobeying him, but something more serious which had to do with my eternal life, he allowed me to go back to class. He told me I could not graduate because of my absences. I hoped this would not be the case. God had proved He was with me, and this increased my faith in Him and my determination to be faithful to Him in all circumstances.

3

Strengthened by His Word

Your words were found and I ate them,
And Your word was to me the joy and rejoicing of my heart;
For I am called by Your name,
O Lord God of hosts.

—Jeremiah 15:16, NKJV

While studying at ITIG,* I knew I could not stay and finish high school there. Even though the school principal had agreed to let me continue my school year, it soon became clear to me that this was only for a short while. All along, my grades had been the best in the class, but to my surprise, at the end of the year, my transcript indicated that I had failed and was therefore not qualified for promotion to a higher level. The report showed that I had been dismissed from the school.

I was somehow prepared to leave although I did not know where to go. I was taking general mechanics courses, and, to my knowledge, there was no other school in the region where I could continue my program. I wondered what would happen next—when God brought about a solution. Someone told me that the Seventh-day Adventist Church had a school with just such a program about 483 kilometers (300 miles) from the city of Goma, in a place called Lukanga.

I went to the same church leaders who had intervened for me with the principal. They quickly arranged for my admission to the school in Lukanga so I could continue my studies there. The only problem was that the school

---

* "Institut Technique Industriel de Goma," the name of one of the high schools in Goma city.

was very expensive, and it would be difficult for me to pay the tuition. It wasn't long, however, before I realized that God had made all the necessary provisions for me to go to Lukanga. A cousin I had never met before, who was living in Kigali, Rwanda, offered to pay for me, and that settled the matter.

During my stay in Lukanga, in the Congo, I went home to Rwanda for school holidays from the first part of August to the end of September 1990. Just about a week later, while I was back in school at Lukanga, war erupted in Rwanda between the government and the Rwandan Patriotic Front (RPF).

The RPF was a group of Rwandans, mainly Tutsis, who had been expelled from the country in 1959 by Hutu revolutionists under the influence of Belgian colonial rule. They had been staying as refugees in neighboring countries. For several years, they had negotiated in vain for a peaceful return. Now, they were attempting to come back, armed, to their home country after about thirty years.

While I was at school in Lukanga and soon after the war broke out, I learned that many Tutsis had been arrested or killed in Rwanda. I also received a letter from one of my friends in Rwanda informing me that some of my relatives had disappeared or been imprisoned. I longed to go home to see for myself. But there was no way I could return to see my family without endangering my life.

By the end of 1990, more and more Rwandans were becoming refugees in neighboring countries. Many young people found themselves separated from their parents, unable to go to school. I was grateful not only to be in school, but to be in the school of my choice, Lukanga Adventist School. However, I was going through a serious financial crisis. I was not paying my school fees because I could no longer receive money from home and had no other source of income.

While I was in Lukanga, the Lord was preparing me for the worst situations that could ever happen. I was enjoying my religious freedom, and I was also interacting with many pastors and young people who knew God and talked about Him all the time. I understood the value of studying in a boarding school where we could sing, pray, and read the Word of God every morning and evening.

I read several books during this time that helped me spiritually. Some of the books that most encouraged my faith were by a writer named Ellen G. White. Books like *Steps to Christ*, *The Great Controversy*, *Early Writings*, *Testimonies*

Strengthened by His Word

for the Church, and others were of great help to me. Mr. and Mrs. Kamberg, who were missionaries in this area, had recommended those writings. I still value those books, along with the Bible, and would recommend them to anyone who wants to build a meaningful, personal relationship with God.

While I was totally disconnected from home, I could find relief only by reading the Word of God and those books. I read for several hours every evening and especially on Sabbath afternoons.

I had a friend with whom I would spend time reading and discussing different books as we pondered what they meant for our lives. Since I could not go back to Rwanda, I also used all my vacation time reading the Word of God and the books mentioned above.

Soon, the dean of men chose me to be in charge of the spiritual life activities among my colleagues. I was organizing morning and evening worship services. People sometimes excused themselves from their preaching commitments, so I often took over and preached most of the time.

In my last year of high school, another difficulty developed. Congo passed a new law requiring all foreign students to pay an examination fee of $150. Since I had no communication with home, the school had tolerated the fact that I could not pay the tuition for a while. But this law now presented a challenge since I did not have the $150 and the school was not ready to pay the fee for me.

This was a serious problem, because it meant I would not be allowed to take the examination and therefore could not graduate from high school. The school principal, who knew what was going on, suggested that I should look into getting a Congolese National Identity Card. The principal's suggestion seemed to be a solution during the few minutes I sat in his office, but as soon as I left and thought about it further, I realized it would involve a lie, a violation of God's principle of truthfulness. I knew I was Rwandan and reasoned that it was not right to lie about being Congolese, just because I wanted to solve an immediate financial problem.

I returned to the principal's office to inform him that I could not do as he'd suggested, because it violated my principles. If I lied to get the identity card, then my dismissal from my former school would have been for no purpose. The principal's reasoning was that, in time of crisis, one has to find any solution. He then offered to be the one to make all the arrangements if I would agree. All I needed to do was to give him my passport pictures. When he realized I was not open to this suggestion, he gave up on me, concluding that I was an extremist.

Things were getting worse. I knew there was nowhere I could get the money. I wondered if I had spent all six years of my high school education in vain since I lacked the $150 needed to take the exam. As I pondered my situation, not knowing what to do next, God was ready to work a miracle.

Karekezi, a Rwandan student in a lower class whom I didn't know, had heard about my dilemma from another source. One morning, after cafeteria time, he told me he had one hundred dollars to give me. According to him, his sponsor had sent him the money to pay for his room and board at school and for restaurant food. He said he would find a decent place to stay with a family in the village so he could attend school as a day student.

Not long afterward, my roommate Greg's mother came to visit him. Upon learning of my financial situation, she gave me fifty dollars, which was the balance I needed for my examination fee. In a few more days, a younger student came and handed me a bunch of money wrapped up in a handkerchief. It was about fifty dollars. She suggested that I keep the money for her. After about two weeks, I asked if she needed her money back. She said she had heard of my need and was giving me that money, although she had intended to use it to pay the remaining balance of her tuition. I tried to reject the offer, but she said this was her decision and that she was even ready to go back home and wait for me to pay her back once I finished my studies.

What this young lady did was amazing. I had no special ties with her to cause her to be willing to give me money. It moved me to see how God could intervene so quickly, bringing people that I had never thought about to help meet my need. Now, I just had to decide who needed their money returned more than the others so I could give back fifty dollars to that person, because I now had more than enough to pay the examination fee.

I prepared to write the final examinations. However, three days before I was to take them, I became very ill. I had a serious nose bleed accompanied by excessive vomiting. I realized, unless God performed another miracle, I would not be able to sit for the examinations.

On Monday morning, I woke up early and went to the examination center. I was still bleeding and had brought two handkerchiefs to help me manage the blood. However, my handkerchiefs became so soiled that I had to leave the room about every twenty minutes. With such an inconvenience it was quite a challenge for me to remain focused. Despite all the problems, I passed my examinations and scored higher than anyone else in my school program.

After completing my examinations, I had no reason to remain at school. I wanted to go home to Rwanda, but I knew it was risky, and I had no money. My sister invited me to stay with her in her home in Goma. I continued to pray and hoped that God would provide me with some money.

The morning after completing my high school national exams, I met a pastor whom I knew well. He informed me he had some news for me. I wondered what it could be. He told me that someone he had met in Rwanda had given him money for me. He then handed me an envelope full of paper money! It was about eighty thousand Congolese francs! He also gave me the equivalent of fifty dollars in Rwandan francs.

The eighty thousand was not a large amount; it was also worth approximately fifty dollars. But in my situation, where I could not easily get even five dollars and having spent about two years with no news from home and no money, it was a lot! This was an answer from God. I could not think of anyone who would have thought to give me money. Strangely, nor could the pastor recall who had given him the money. Instead of worrying about who this person might be, I thanked God for answering my prayers.

With money in my pocket, I could think of going back home in September 1992. I went to stay at my sister's house in Goma for a week or two. Finally, I dared to cross the border, knowing that I was taking a big risk with my life. I was missing my family, and I needed to see them. I went straight to Kigali, not knowing what to expect.

When I arrived in Kigali, I met a few friends who gave me a warm welcome and updated me on what had happened during my absence. In no time at all, I was part of the life of my former local church again. Soon I was elected to be one of the church elders at the tender age of twenty-two years. I received many preaching appointments in and around Kigali. News of the atrocities occurring around the region kept multiplying, but the Word of God was my comfort, and because I was busy preaching, it seemed like nothing unusual was happening.

In March 1994, I went to my home village for the weekend. There I met my father, five sisters, and one brother. I was glad to visit each home and see my nephews, nieces, and other relatives again. My visit was very memorable. In fact, these are the most important memories I still have of my family. We had a lot of discussions about what had happened during the long period of separation, trying to update each other on events and experiences. We did not sense that this was the last time we would get together in this life.

After some time with my family, they bid me farewell as I left for Kigali. My plans were to return home again in July of the same year.

Things were changing. One politician after another began to die mysteriously. In Kigali, thousands of young people were receiving military training and being given weapons and uniforms. I could not get a full sense of what was going on. Meanwhile, every night, some people were being attacked and killed in their homes because of their ethnic background or for political reasons.

During this period, there was a new radio station that was spreading hate propaganda. Hutus were told not only to despise their Tutsi neighbors, but to regard them as enemies and dangerous people. These messages of hate flooded the airwaves. The radio played revolutionary songs all day and all night. Hate-based political movements recruited young people. They enticed those who initially refused to join the gangs with incentives such as jobs, driver's licenses, and money. Over the radio, these movements often invited the youth to urgent meetings, mostly held at night.

While all this was going on, Christians in small group meetings discussed political involvement. Partisanship was being discouraged. So far, the problem was at the recruitment level. The killings involved only trained groups. Such activities were still considered crimes, at least by the common people.

In the church, there seemed to be no apparent problem between Hutus and Tutsis. They were worshiping side by side. Neighbors shared what they had, and marriages between Hutus and Tutsis still occurred. But with widespread reports of killings, fear erupted. People were trying to move out of the city in fear of the militia, who often came at night and killed entire families.

During this time, I traveled across the country, preaching in several churches and conducting evangelistic programs. I was also attending small group prayer meetings, in which church members met one day during the week to pray for their spiritual well-being and for God's protection. We felt we were living in the last days, and no one knew what would happen. The killings continued, but we believed Jesus would come soon. Thousands and thousands of people were praying, while others were being trained to slaughter their neighbors.

Strengthened by His Word

At the end of March 1994, I had just finished an evangelistic effort in the Lycee de Kicukiro in Kigali, where I had gotten a teaching job in early 1993. A fellow teacher had decided to become a Christian and was baptized along with twenty-four students.

I will never forget Charles. He was one of the youths to whom I had preached. Others had been baptized, but Charles hadn't because his father refused to grant him permission to do so. I remember talking to him prior to the baptismal service as he sobbed uncontrollably. His father simply did not want him to be baptized, and all his mother's efforts to make his father understand were futile. I asked Charles to make a difficult decision. I told him he needed to choose between obeying his father or God. This was his dilemma. He went back home and tried to convince his father one more time, but in vain. Charles did not get baptized, and he would never have the chance to make this decision for baptism again.

After the evangelistic effort at Lycee de Kicukiro, we began the Easter holidays, and schools were closed. Many young people were gathering for prayer. I was invited twice that week, prior to the genocide, to speak at such gatherings. On Tuesday, we consecrated the whole day for prayer in one church member's home. I had an opportunity to strengthen the young people who feared for their possible impending doom.

During our meeting, many reported that there had been some attacks in their neighborhoods and that they were staying outside their homes at night. After some discussion, we prayed for protection as we faced a future that was becoming more and more uncertain. After the day of prayer, we felt convinced that God could save our lives no matter what might happen. We also affirmed in our hearts that should anything happen, the most serious problem we faced was that one might not be found ready for eternal life.

On Wednesday, I had another appointment with a small group of fellow church members. They had similar concerns over the worsening political situation. I gave them some words of encouragement and concluded our meeting with a prayer for God's will to prevail as we faced the worsening crisis.

4

Declaration of Identity

God is our refuge and strength,
an ever-present help in trouble.
Therefore we will not fear, though the earth give way
and the mountains fall into the heart of the sea,
though its waters roar and foam
and the mountains quake with their surging.
—Psalm 46:1–3

On the evening of April 6, 1994, calamity fell upon Rwanda. I had been praying with a group of friends throughout the day. On my return home, I went by the house of my church's first elder to ask him about some matters concerning our church. To my amazement, after just a few minutes of conversation, an unusual sense of danger came over him, and he asked me to go home immediately.

As he went with me to the fence surrounding his house, we saw something that looked like a huge shooting star toward the eastern part of the city. It lasted much longer than the normal phenomenon of a shooting star. In reality, it was the plane carrying Juvénal Habyarimana, the president of Rwanda, and Cyprien Ntaryamira, the president of Burundi. Their plane had just been shot down. The two presidents were coming from the Tanzanian capital, Dar es Salaam, for a power-sharing summit between the government of Rwanda and the Rwandan Patriotic Front.

As soon as I arrived home, I heard a public announcement on national radio that no one was to leave their house until further notice from the appropriate civil authorities. We spent the whole night in prayer, thinking the situation would soon become normal. Meanwhile, shootings were intensifying across the city. Every single home was being visited and searched by the government army and the militiamen as they sought to kill Tutsis.

It was impossible for anyone in the city of Kigali to go to church on the morning of April 9, 1994, because people were being killed everywhere, and the militia had put roadblocks on every street. Instead of risking walking to our church building some two kilometers (one mile) away, I invited my neighbors to my house for a prayer meeting. We were all afraid of what was going on. A few people came, and by nine o'clock we started our meeting.

For our meditation, I selected a chapter entitled, "The Time of Trouble" from the book, *The Great Controversy* by Ellen G. White. I thought this was a relevant subject, taking into account the atrocities that were going on in our country. I was leading out at the prayer meeting. My purpose was to draw the attention of the fearful group to the fact that God has promised to be with His people even during the time of their severest trials. Referring to the experience of Jacob, who wrestled with the Angel until He blessed him,[1] I suggested that we wrestle with God in prayer. I reminded the people that He would be our shield in such a time of trouble.

While I was reading and relating the passages to our immediate life experience, there was a sudden interruption. Six armed militiamen entered the gate to my house. They knocked vehemently, shouting angrily. I could see them through the glass of the front door. Since there was no other way out, my house-helper opened the door for them as they kept shouting and threatening to fire their weapons. We were all asked to remain seated as they surrounded us.

"IDs out!" commanded one who appeared to be the leader of the group.

Among our group, some were Tutsis and others were not. The Tutsis had thrown away their IDs since the cards would show who they were and cause their death. The Hutus showed their IDs, and I pretended to show mine too. Reaching into my back pocket, I presented my residential permit since it had no ethnic identification on it. But the permit looked different, and it instantly caught the attention of the man who was standing closest to me. He snatched it from my hand and demanded that I show them my national ID card. I knew I was in deep trouble. I then quickly, yet reluctantly, pulled out my Tutsi ID from my shirt pocket. I handed it to him, fully aware of what doing so would mean. They were looking for Tutsis to kill, and now I would be their next victim.

Declaration of Identity

As soon as the militiaman found out I was Tutsi, he announced his discovery to the others with great excitement. "Get ready to kill!" he shouted.

Immediately all the men raised their machetes over my head and awaited the signal to cut me to pieces. For a moment I felt numb. I was now the center of everyone's attention. Meanwhile, the militiamen did not search the rest of the people in the group and appeared to forget about them. There was no evidence to prove they were Tutsis, but at least they had found one. I kept praying silently for God to do something about the situation. The militiamen were now blaming my friends for having sympathized with a Tutsi whom, they said, they should consider their enemy. To save their own lives, most of them said they had not known I was a Tutsi.

Then suddenly, with machetes still raised above my head, I felt a strong urge to say something. I sensed some strange power in me as I raised my head to face the man who had just given the order. Quickly, and with unusual boldness, I held up my Bible and firmly declared, "On that ID is written, 'Tutsi,' but on my heart is written, 'Citizen of Heaven.' "

The commander of the militia snatched the Bible from my hand. With terrible anger, he threw it down and trampled on it. As this happened, I closed my eyes again and hung my head in disappointment. I prayed, "Lord, I thought You would fight for me in such a moment, but now You are being despised, and they are trampling on Your Word! Won't You do something?"

I believed that God would act. He was still God, and He was in control! Everyone sat frozen in fear. The machetes were still hovering over my head, ready to strike, but no one would say a word. Drunk with the blood of the many people he had already killed, the commander now stood before a God who controls through unseen means. While the commander shouted unceasingly, I kept praying. Then, suddenly, there was a shift in focus.

"Take us to your bedroom," the commander ordered, motioning for me to get up.

As I stood and led him to my bedroom, I thought, *He has decided to kill me away from the rest of my friends and neighbors.* Walking into the room, I put everything into God's hands. My prayer was simple and straightforward: "Lord, stand by my side now." As we entered, two of the commander's colleagues joined him, and they began scrambling for my few possessions. They took all the pairs of shoes they could find, five thousand Rwandan francs (the equivalent of fifteen dollars), and anything else they found useful. Then they brought me out of the bedroom and back to the sitting room where everyone else had remained. My friends were surprised to see me return still alive.

As the drama continued to unfold, I silently prayed with every breath, aware that unless God protected me, these men could snuff out my life at any minute. Unexpectedly, the commander of the militia then began to address the whole group in a manner that suggested he was mentally disturbed. Meanwhile, I continued to stand surrounded by angry killers who were just waiting for the final order to kill. My friends were speechless, not knowing whether they would be killed along with me.

Finally, instead of giving the order to kill me (which the militiamen were looking forward to), the commander looked at me with piercing eyes and said, "We will not kill you. Instead, we will call the Presidential Guard (the elite segment of the Rwanda National Army) to come and burn you alive."

As soon as he said this, one of his men, who was not happy with this decision, quickly raised his knife and with all his might stabbed me twice in my head, between my right ear and the top of my head. I cannot explain what happened! I expected to be bleeding profusely. But I felt nothing serious. Not even the wound! There was only a droplet of blood in my hair. The Lord had worked a miracle and shielded me from the stabbing that was meant to end my life.

As the momentum to kill slackened, and they lowered their machetes one after another, the commander ordered me to hand him my house keys. I knew God had answered my prayers. This group had killed other people in the community, and our house was just the next in line. There was no reason for them not to have killed me and my friends—except that God had miraculously intervened.

Using my house keys, they locked us inside the house. As soon as they left, we knelt down to pray as a group. We thanked God for the miracles He had performed before our eyes. We entrusted our immediate future into His hands, fully aware that the Presidential Guard would be coming shortly to burn us alive as promised. I resumed teaching the group from the same book, *The Great Controversy,* continuing with the same chapter on the "Time of Trouble." Most of the people could no longer concentrate on what I was saying. They were visibly shaken by what had happened. One lady suggested that instead of teaching, I should let them pray individually while awaiting the Presidential Guard's arrival. I consented.

Declaration of Identity

About an hour had passed when a young girl, about ten years old, knocked at the door of my house. We didn't know what to expect. She slid my house keys through the gap under the door. When I opened the door for her, she explained that she had met the six militiamen walking down the road. They told her to bring the keys to us. Her mother was one of our group.

No sooner had the young girl and her mother left for their home than the rest of my neighbors also decided to return to their own homes. I respected their decisions, but urged them to continue praying. I now remained with my two friends, Jules, who was a Hutu, and Paul, who was a Tutsi, and a young boy, Toto, a Hutu who was working for us as a house-helper.

The time was now around noon. After thanking God for what had happened, my friends and I went outside the house to stretch our legs after such a stressful and terrifying time. We had walked barely a few meters when we saw the same militia commander, armed with a pistol and a big knife, approaching the gate of my house. We knew trouble had returned. We retreated into the house quickly. I grabbed my Bible, and we tried to escape through the back door and over the fence on that side of the house. We jumped the fence, only to be met by a group of militiamen who had already encircled the house. These were the same men who had come to my house to kill me some hours earlier. This time they were determined to kill me at all costs. There was no place to run. I had but one option: pray to God for His miraculous protection. The men ordered me to lie down on my stomach while they waited for their commander who was coming through the front gate. In the meantime, the rest of the militia closed in on me.

Finally, the commander arrived with his fury going before him. Since I was lying on my stomach, I could not see him approach, but I could hear him shouting and cursing as he came. I knew he was about to kill me.

"I'm going to cut your throat!" he shouted as he came closer. I heard him pull his big knife from the sheath on his side and felt its pointed tip touch my throat. Right as the blade was about to touch my throat, a strange surge of power and courage coursed through my body. I raised my Bible, which I was firmly holding to my chest, pointed it at him and cried, "Don't spill innocent blood!"

He immediately withdrew the knife from my throat. He became agitated and acted crazy, as if something mysterious had hit him. He threw away the knife, raised both of his hands, and shouted at me. It was as though he seemed threatened. He continued saying a lot of senseless words for an extended period as one who had lost his mind. All eyes were on him. His subordinates clearly wondered what had happened to him.

Amid this confusion, I was witnessing another remarkable miracle. I believe that God had stepped in during this time when I needed Him most! As I recall this experience, my faith grows even stronger, and I know that if it were not for the Lord, my life could have ended right then.

While the commander shouted in his confusion, Paul and Jules sat motionless a few meters away. No one was saying anything to them. They were astonished and didn't know what to say or what would happen. Fearing the killers would turn on them, they remained still, lest any movement attract attention in their direction. Obviously, I was the target of the militia, and they were too preoccupied with determining my fate to think about anyone else.

After a few minutes, the commander said accusingly, "Why were you running away if you are not an accomplice and consider yourself blameless? Stand up and go back to your house."

"I will not run again," I said while standing up and returning to my house with Paul and Jules. My would-be killers stood speechless.

We closed the door behind us, fell on our knees, and thanked God. We praised Him for preserving our lives one more time.

At about 3:00 P.M., the same commander of the militia came back. I guess he was on another killing mission, heading toward a destination known only to himself and his companions. But this time his heart had turned favorable toward me. He was like a friend, and he called from the door without entering the house, "*Murokore* (devoted one), are you in? You are not hiding any Tutsis in there, are you?"

"I am here," I replied.

There we were, apparently defenseless, but God had built a wall of protection around my house. The killers would now skip my house without harming us as they searched our neighborhood for other Tutsis to kill. Thousands of people were being killed in Kigali. Even for me, the threat was not over. My friends and I seized the opportunity during this short period of peace to thank God for protecting us and prayed for calm to return to our troubled country.

I was not the only one whom some militiamen had nicknamed, "*Murokore.*" I remember one Tutsi, a fellow church member, well-known in his

Declaration of Identity

neighborhood for his kindness. When the genocide broke out, the militia refused to touch him or his family. All the militiamen commissioned to kill him remembered his goodness and refrained from taking his life. At one time, two Tutsis, a boy aged nine, and a girl aged seven, came to his home seeking refuge after militiamen had killed their parents. He took them in. The militia pursued them all the way to his home. Yet when they arrived, they inquired the same way the militia commander had inquired of me, "*Murokore*, are you hiding any Tutsis?"

"No," he replied.

"All along we thought you were a saint, but now you're lying. We saw the two children come into your house!" the killers asserted.

The man admitted the truth and explained how sorry he was for having lied. He tried to reason with them, insisting that if they themselves were the ones seeking refuge in his house, he would have hidden them the same way he had hidden these children. He pleaded in vain for their lives. The killers told him that if he had not lied to them, they would have spared the children. The "holy" man's lie had disappointed them, they claimed, and as his punishment, they killed the boy and left only the girl alive.

---

1. Ellen G. White, *The Great Controversy* (Mountain View, CA: Pacific Press®, 1950), 616.

5

Treading the Deadly Path

"Be strong and of good courage, do not fear nor be afraid
of them; for the LORD your God, He is the One who
goes with you. He will not leave you nor forsake you."
—Deuteronomy 31:6, NKJV

During the evening of April 13, the militia announced that nobody was to sleep in their homes that night. Everyone was to join the militia in patrolling the streets until dawn. There had been rumors that the Rwanda Patriotic Army (RPA)* was approaching. Because of my Tutsi ID, I was afraid to leave my house, and besides, I was not even supposed to go out. To them, I was a Tutsi, a traitor, just another candidate for death. I had to wait in my house, but my two friends, Paul and Jules, went. The militia made everyone line up along the road and commanded them to remain vigilant. They wanted to use the people as shields against the approaching army.

Around midnight, according to what my friends told me later, they saw a group of soldiers marching on the street before them. Their military attire differed from the ones they were familiar with. They were RPA soldiers passing by. The militia and the group of people with them hid among the bushes until the soldiers had marched past.

After the soldiers had gone, the militia became furious. They gathered together all the people they had asked to watch with them throughout the night. They told them things had changed and ordered everybody to return to their homes and wait.

---

* "Rwanda Patriotic Army" (RPA) was a name for the combatant forces of the Rwandan Patriotic Front (RPF).

Preaching From the Grave

"Tomorrow, early in the morning, we are coming to kill all the Tutsis who are still alive. We will spare no one!" they emphasized.

Paul and Jules returned to my house after midnight. As they entered, they seemed troubled, tired, and terrified. I asked them how things had gone, but they would not say a word. I became suspicious. Studying their faces, I suspected something terrible was about to happen. I kept on urging them to tell me what was going on, but they remained silent.

I knew they were worried about my fate and did not dare to tell me any dreadful news. After asking them at least three times and making no progress, I was becoming unhappy with them.

"Brother Jules, don't you know me?" I asked. "Do you think I will lose all hope in God now? Do you think God will forsake me now, after He has seen me through all the difficulties I have been through?"

After hearing my intense frustration, Jules realized there was no reason to keep quiet. He paused and then said, "We won't hide it from you any longer. We had decided not to tell you this, but since you insist, we will tell you now. Tomorrow, the militia is coming to kill you. They clearly stated that they will spare no Tutsi."

In view of what my friends had divulged, I remarked, "Even if the whole army comes to kill me, they won't succeed unless God allows them to. They will not kill me. Let us ask God to be in charge of the situation."

They consented, and we began to pray. Our prayer took a simple format. We each took turns praying and paused for reflection at intervals. We recounted what God had already done for us in the past few days and poured out our hearts to Him.

However, as we prayed, my friend Paul did not say a word. I thought he was so troubled that he had no courage to pray. He remained silent for two or three hours while Jules and I kept praying. After those hours of silence, he said a prayer that was unique. It was unlike all the prayers we had been praying. He taught me a lesson for a lifetime, which I will never forget.

He prayed, "Lord, the French government has rescued its citizens. The Americans have also taken away their people. The Belgians have rescued their own. We know that we are Your people. There are types of food we do not eat and beverages we do not drink. There are schools we do not attend, because we are not of this world. Now, evil people surround us, and we have nowhere to go. Are You not more powerful than the Americans or the French? Lord, come and save Your people."

This prayer, and how it was answered, convinced me that the God we serve is indeed God. He can answer and rescue when we pray.

After much prayer, we all became convinced that God was in control and that nothing would happen to us outside of His will. We could not sleep that night, because we did not want to face an attack unprepared. At dawn, as I was sitting on my bed meditating in my heart and saying silent prayers, I heard a shout. Someone was hitting our gate very hard and calling out with a harsh voice, demanding that we allow him to come in.

"Open! I will burn you in that house!" he shouted.

I expected my friend Paul to go open the gate, since they were looking for me, but he was too scared to move. We all thought the militia had come according to the evil plan they had made the previous night.

Paul shouted, "I will open for you! I am getting dressed."

But he was so shaken that he could not take even one step. As a result, he continued to delay and didn't go to open the gate. He just kept nervously moving in the same small space as if in a cage. Meanwhile, I was busy praying, asking God to place an angel by our gate so that nobody would come and harm us.

Suddenly, there was a heavy explosion close to my house, followed immediately by complete calm and peace. Later, someone told us that the shouting militiaman was shot and had run for his life. All I know is that the militia did not come. Again, God had extended His protection over us and calmed the raging sea.

We had been spared and were grateful, but another drama was unfolding. After sunrise, we saw many people from the surrounding areas gathering close to our house. It was obvious that they were running away from the locations where the fighting was fiercest. They came in search of refuge and found an empty, tall building close to my house. That building actually was no refuge at all, because eventually all the people hiding there were brutally killed. From my house, I could see them being thrown out of windows from several floors up. The militia waited at the foot of the building to cut into pieces those who were not dead after hitting the ground.

Within days, everything had changed dramatically. The militia had killed thousands of Tutsis in Kigali. They also killed some moderate Hutus, mostly politicians, who were not supportive of the government barbarisms against Tutsis. People ran here and there, and fear was everywhere. One of my church members, Pierre, who was a Hutu, came to my house to see if I was still alive. He brought me some cookies, sensing I had not been eating for days. It amazed him to hear about how God had preserved our lives.

Pierre suggested that we flee to another province. I considered the option, but realized that my Tutsi ID card would complicate things for me. Pierre asked me to tear it up, but I refused. I told him I would not lie by disguising my identity and saying I was a Hutu. I declared that it was God who had saved me in the past, not an ID card or any action on my part. I decided that I would rather die while remaining honest than lie to live.

When Pierre realized that I was not giving in and that there was nothing else he could do, he looked straight into my eyes and said, "If you have that kind of faith, then let's go!"

I asked my friends to come together for prayer, and then with my Tutsi ID in my hands, we started our journey.

Since both Jules and Pierre were originally from Gitarama, Pierre thought we would find safety there, staying with their parents. He suggested that we leave Kigali and flee to the southern province of Gitarama where he thought it would be peaceful.

Pierre's brother, Samson, joined us. We were now six, including our house-helper, Toto. We were ready to tread the deadly path ahead of us. I packed some of my belongings, which consisted of a few books, a big portable radio, and some clothes. One of my friends carried the books, and I took the radio. My intention was to cover my face with it to avoid being noticed by the killers who could often judge one's ethnic background from afar just by looking at one's face.

Sensing the dangers ahead due to my identity, Pierre had devised a plan that would take me through the city of Kigali, since going to Gitarama required crossing through Kigali. As we started the journey, he asked for my ID card and placed it under his. His strategy was that if anyone asked us to produce our IDs, Pierre would go first and show his Hutu ID. Then when my turn came, he would say he had my card and would come back and show them his ID card again.

We began our journey through Kigali on Friday, April 15, around nine o'clock in the morning. The way was long, not because of the distance, but

Treading the Deadly Path

because of the many roadblocks and events that hampered our progress. At each of these roadblocks, and even in between them, there were ID card checks by the militia who were bent on eliminating anyone with a card that said "Tutsi" on it.

As we left my house, there was nowhere to hide and no way to move safely. All around us, people were being killed just because they were Tutsis. I walked about two hundred meters with no one noticing me until we reached the first roadblock.

As I saw the armed killers and the people they told to wait to one side, I prayed in my heart that God would help us pass this first roadblock safely. Pierre used his strategy. He approached the killer who wanted to see his ID. Upon seeing it had Hutu written on it, he let Pierre pass and then asked me to produce my ID. I told the militiaman that Pierre, who had now walked ahead, had my ID.

"I have his card!" Pierre declared as he came back showing his own ID card again. The militiaman did not even read it but gave the signal to allow me to pass through. I had been spared. As I walked past, I recognized some people who had been ordered to sit down. They were waiting to be killed. My heart filled with terror.

They detained Paul at this roadblock and made him stand among those that would soon die. Pierre went back to negotiate his release, leaving me to continue on with Jules, Samson, and Toto. Paul had been held back, because he didn't have an ID card. On April 6, after the broadcast about the death of the president, Paul had torn up his Tutsi ID card, because many Tutsis were being killed. So, now he could not go through the roadblock. The militia wanted him to produce an ID, but he had none. Sadly, we had to leave him behind. There was nothing the rest of us could do to help our friend.

Only a hundred meters down the road, Jules, Samson, Toto, and I approached another roadblock. I should mention it was very difficult to continue without Pierre, who had helped me pass through the previous roadblock. Before we left him and Paul, he had given me back my ID card. Before reaching this next roadblock, I stopped for a while and thought about returning to my house, but even back there, people were being killed. The only option was to advance, because going back would also mean death and staying in one place would attract the militia's attention.

As we proceeded, we were appalled by the many dead people we saw on either side of the road. Then, as we approached the militia, I pleaded with God. "Lord, close their eyes in Jesus' name!"

As soon as I said this prayer, God intervened! The militiamen seemed distracted, and I moved ahead with no one asking any questions.

I said this prayer several times at different roadblocks, and God answered right away. I remember coming across one roadblock and seeing a militiaman leaning against a street sign. He was smoking something that I suspect must have been marijuana, because it did not look like any kind of cigarette I had seen before. I knew that he, too, would want to see my ID card. Instantly, I whispered a prayer—the same prayer: "Lord, close his eyes in the name of Jesus." When I got to him, he asked me for my ID card and I gave it to him. As he tried to open my ID, his hands were shaking as if he was sick. He kept struggling to open my ID while looking at my face.

He then asked, "Don't you communicate with these rebels?"

"No!" I replied.

He handed back my ID card and allowed Samson, Jules, Toto, and me to proceed. Another miracle had taken place, and I thanked God that he had closed the eyes of this militiaman.

After about fifty meters, we came upon a different kind of roadblock. This was just a chaotic group of people blocking the road. Many were asking for IDs and many were busy producing them. I knew they would also require me to produce my ID. Jules and Toto did not have a problem, because they had Hutu IDs, and Samson was too young to have one, so no one ever bothered him.

This time the situation was unimaginable. There were a lot of militiamen—more than twenty, as I recall—and every one of them was checking IDs, searching for Tutsis to kill. I prayed the same prayer, again and again, asking God to close their eyes as I moved through the busy crowd of killers and their victims. As I moved along, every militiaman was busy with someone else, checking IDs. No one ever asked me to show mine, probably thinking the killer beyond him would deal with me. I sneaked through the crowd, holding my ID until I passed the last killer. God was proving He was in control.

However, the series of roadblocks was far from over. About another hundred meters down the road, I came to yet another roadblock. Confident that God would not let me down, I prayed, "Close their eyes in Jesus' name!" But the first person to see me asked for my ID. I gave it to him. When he read

Treading the Deadly Path

"Tutsi" on my ID, he could not believe I was still holding such a deadly card. "Are you Tutsi?" he whispered. "Disappear!" He pressed the card back into my hand, and I walked ahead. God had answered my prayer again! As I think back about what happened, I feel God was telling me that His answers were not only about closing the eyes of the killers. He was teaching me that He could save my life, even when the militiaman knew who I was. He never runs out of options!

I didn't run, because that would have aroused suspicion. When we'd moved on only about ten meters, a truck full of militiamen arrived at that roadblock. All those manning the roadblock shifted their attention to the men in this truck. Meanwhile, the militiaman who had told me to disappear called me back. He told the driver of the truck to give us a ride. When the driver resisted, the militiaman informed him that unless he complied with his demand, the truck would not be moving on. I was praying and wondering what was going on. All eyes were looking at me while I pretended to have no problem. I still feared they would discover who I was by looking at my face.

The other militiamen must have suspected I was a Tutsi, because they asked my protector accusingly, "Are we fighting ourselves?" But he paid no attention to what they were saying. Instead, he grabbed me with my radio on my head and threw me into the vehicle. My two friends and Toto also followed and jumped into the truck. We were now among the killers in the truck, all with long knives and grenades. As I listened to them talking, I discovered that they were coming from a killing mission in the Gikondo area, a suburb next to mine.

As the vehicle moved forward, I realized that God had given us a short break and protected us from going through one of the most dreadful scenes. We had gone only a short distance when I began seeing dead people—and some who were in the process of dying—piled on either side of the road. Many others were scattered all over. When I saw this horrible picture, I felt terribly disheartened. Realizing that my panicked appearance would attract the militiamen's attention, I tried to calm myself and looked down to avoid causing the killers to question who I was and kill me at any moment.

Soon the vehicle left the main road and entered a compound in Kiyovu. We arrived at what looked to be the home of the chief militiaman in the group. He seemed troubled as he announced, "We will kill in Gitarama area, and every one of you must get a gun." My two friends and I were now part of the militia group! I had no idea would happen to us next. After a few minutes, the chief militiaman noticed us and remembered we were strangers. He shouted, "You! Get out of my compound!"

Without hesitation, we left and headed back to the highway, fearing that something else would happen to us. God had arranged this short ride for us, thereby preventing us from experiencing the horrific death that would have been ours. But our journey was not even half over as we attempted to cross the city.

Before we reached the main road, we met a large group of people who also seemed to be running away. They were walking in the opposite direction. I heard them speaking in Swahili. Having lived in Congo over six years, I could tell from their features that they were Congolese. I asked them where they were going. They gave me a rude response.

"Sisi tuna kwenda ku ambassade yetu! (We are going to our embassy!)" they replied. They showed by their tone and facial expressions that they wanted nothing to do with me or my friends. When we first saw them, we had thought of joining their group as they made their way to their embassy. But it was clear they did not wish to be associated with us, so we let them go by as we proceeded to the main road.

6

Fighting Beside the Dead

*"Thus says the L*ORD* who made it, the L*ORD* who formed it to establish it (the L*ORD* is His name): 'Call to Me, and I will answer you, and show you great and mighty things, which you do not know.'"*
—Jeremiah 33:2, 3, NKJV

Once we reached the highway, Jules, Samson, Toto, and I looked behind and in front of us. There was no safe place. We were speechless as we saw all the roadblocks in each direction. My friends were worried about me. They had seen many of God's miracles, but we were about to face the worst roadblocks still ahead.

I was tired and lacked the strength to stand. But I could not sit either. The militia was everywhere, and I had to make sure no one around noticed that I was a Tutsi. I resolved to pray again and entreat God to carry me on His wings!

Not too long after praying this prayer, I saw Pierre and Paul coming toward us from down the road! The last time we had seen them was six or seven hours earlier, when we had left Paul detained at the roadblock where he had failed to produce an ID card. Pierre had risked his life to remain with him and negotiate his release. Miraculously, they had now made it to where we were. Upon seeing me, Pierre and Paul were so surprised, because they thought they had seen my body among some of the dead along the side of the road. With tears in their eyes, they praised God that we were alive and reunited.

The journey ahead seemed terrible. We all felt discouraged and in constant fear for our lives. Toto had been going through all the hardships we experienced. He did not want to continue to associate with us. There was

Preaching From the Grave

a Roman Catholic church near the highway where people were running to seek safety. He said he wanted to go there. I knew it was not a safe place since the militiamen regarded nothing as sacred. Toto knew this, too, but since he was a Hutu, he may have felt it was better than facing the same dangers he'd already seen while traveling with us.

Together, we continued to the next roadblock just before the main traffic roundabout in the center of Kigali. The people inspecting ID cards here seemed as ferocious as any of those we had met along the way. It was apparent that more trouble awaited us.

"Lord, close their eyes in Jesus' name!" I prayed as I handed my ID to a militiaman.

This time, God did not seem to close anybody's eyes. As soon as the militiaman read the inscription "Tutsi" on my ID card, he shouted, "We have found one! We have found one!" In a few seconds, a group of fierce-looking men armed with machetes, knives, and grenades surrounded me.

Jules and Samson continued on their way. Paul also made it through. Though a Tutsi, Paul had fooled many by his more Hutu-like facial features. Pierre, a Hutu, was such a faithful friend. Having stayed the whole day negotiating for Paul, he now decided to remain with me as the militiamen were about to kill me. He tried to plead for my release. He even offered them the little money he had. But nothing seemed to touch their hearts or appeal to their selfish interests. In fact, the more he begged for my release, the more irritated they became.

"You are an accomplice!" one man shouted at Pierre and threatened to kill him. The man then chased after him, but Pierre outran him as he fled for his life down a hill going toward the Nyabugogo area. He thus escaped death but had no hope I would survive. As he reached the bottom of the hill, he met up with the rest of our little group and reported my death. But the God whom I had prayed to was in control no matter the circumstances.

After the killers had surrounded me, my situation took a horrible turn. One militiaman ordered me to lie down among the dead, right next to a man they had just killed. I would not lie down. I did not want to die, so I remained standing. I put down the big radio which I had been carrying on my head all along, and prayed, "Lord, the time has come for You to show Your protection. Show them I am Your servant and that You are my God!"

I waited for them to come for me at any moment, but they seemed to have

54

forgotten about me. The increasing traffic of refugees trying to escape for their lives preoccupied the militiamen as they searched for Tutsis to kill. Their delay in coming to kill me gave me time to continue praying. As I prayed, I remained confident that God was in charge, just as He had been in the past.

Then, one militiaman looked to where I was standing.

"We didn't kill that man!" he shouted loud enough for everyone to hear.

With terrible anger, he ran in my direction, waving his long knife, intent on killing me. As he approached, I prayed, "Lord, stop him in Jesus' name!"

When I opened my eyes after this short prayer, I saw the killer, who had been running toward me from about ten meters away, now making a U-turn and going in the opposite direction. It seemed as if something, or someone, had prevented him from getting any closer. I kept standing, thanking God for what had just happened.

God had answered my prayer miraculously. I believe He sent His angel to protect me. Given the fury with which the man had charged me, the only explanation I have for what I saw is that God intervened to guarantee my safety at that critical moment.

More time elapsed, and I remained standing beside the dead, not knowing what to expect. Everybody still seemed caught up with inspecting IDs at the roadblock.

Another militiaman observed that I was still alive after they had already given the order to kill me. He shouted, pointing in my direction, "That man hasn't been killed yet! What's going on here?"

He came toward me with fury, ready to kill me as soon as he could. I knew this was a terrible moment. My hope was in God.

"Lord, stop him in Jesus' name!" I repeated the same prayer as before.

As soon as I finished this plea, I opened my eyes to see this man going the opposite direction, just like the one before him.

By this time, I had no doubt at all that God's power was with me. He had been so merciful and was listening and acting as I prayed. There was no coincidence or chance that could have brought about these miracles, at least not twice in the same way and right after two short prayers. Even now, I am encouraged to believe that there is a God in heaven who acts as a Friend and walks with the humble in spirit.

While it is true that thousands were dying around me, God was still God and acting in Rwanda. Based on what my eyes were seeing, I realized that the same God who had walked with Moses, Elijah, Elisha, and many others in the past, was also walking with me for a purpose. I was and remain grateful to witness God at work.

I thought I was dreaming, but I wasn't. It was real. I was part of this drama, and God was in control. By now I felt greater confidence in God, but my anxiety was still there. The battle was still going on, and I was exhausted. I believed, however, that God was far from forsaking me.

About ten more minutes passed, and I was still standing, awaiting my fate. A third militiaman saw me and reacted the same way the other two had. Once again, the same sequence of events repeated itself. The militiaman wondered why they had not killed me yet and came running toward me. I said the same prayer, asking the Lord to stop him, and as I opened my eyes again, I saw him turning in the opposite direction.

I was thankful to God for what He had been doing for me. He was answering my prayers and intervening as soon as I prayed. But I was wondering if this same scenario would be endless. God seemed to say, "I will show you more!"

I was praying in my heart, standing in the same position near the dead person, when a fourth militiaman saw me and wondered what was going on. "Why are we not killing that boy?" he complained. "I will do it myself!"

He approached, full of anger, with a long knife in his hand, ready to kill me. I believed God would answer my prayer again. "Lord, stop him in Jesus' name!" I prayed the short prayer which had turned away the killers before.

But that was not the case this time. As I opened my eyes, I saw that he was still coming closer. I closed my eyes again and said the same prayer. But when I opened my eyes to see if God had answered, the militiaman was standing right before me with the tip of his knife pointed at my face. He had a strange look in his eyes. There was no time to say another prayer, and I wondered what would happen next.

The man gazed into my eyes and asked, *"Uri muntu ki?"* (What kind of person are you?)

Without thinking, a reply came into my mind, and I said with confidence, "I am a man of God!"

"Are you a man of God? I will get your ID so you can go," he said.

I could not understand what had happened! What had the man seen in my face? Could it be he saw a different being, something strange or supernatural?

Fighting Beside the Dead

Maybe he saw an angel beside me or became confused and felt a kind of terror inside himself so that he did not dare to stab me. These questions are still in my mind even today. I believe and I know, however, that this was nothing like a coincidence. God was right there! Even when I was standing beside the dead, awaiting my death, God was fighting on my behalf.

After a while, the killer came back with the news that the militia had refused to release my card. "Don't you have any money to give those guys so they will give your card back and let you go?" he asked.

"I have none on me," I responded. Pierre had tried to give them money before, and they had refused! How was money going to help me now?

"I'm sorry," he spoke with regret. "There is nothing more I can do to help you."

All along I had been standing on the island of the roundabout, the part around which cars encircle. There were dead people on all sides of me. Across the road, perhaps some twenty meters away from the roadblock where IDs were being checked, sat another man armed with a gun. From the authority he seemed to possess, I concluded that he might be one the leaders of that group of militiamen.

"Tell that boy to come here," he commanded one militiaman.

With my radio in my hands, I made my way across the road to where this "commander" was. He didn't talk to me at first, and I did not go too close to him because of fear. I stood before him and waited for something to happen.

As I was gazing at him and praying in my heart, a man came up behind me and touched my shoulder. As I turned, I recognized him as the same militiaman who had tried to negotiate the release of my ID card but had been unsuccessful.

"Did you say you're a man of God?" he asked.

"Yes!" I responded.

In a strong, authoritative, and angry tone, he continued, "If you're a man of God, why don't you ask for your ID card and leave?"

At that moment a strange feeling came over me. My strength revived and great courage filled my heart. The words this man spoke sounded as if they were spoken by an angel. I believed this was not the killer's idea. It felt like I'd just heard a messenger from God who assured me that if I were His man, I could have power over anyone and anything. All this came to my mind in seconds. Without hesitation and leaving my radio behind, I walked back toward the killers to claim my ID card.

I had taken only a few steps when the man who had called me to come to him from across the roundabout became conscious of my presence again. Until now, he had been silent, but suddenly, I heard him shout, "Give him his ID card and let him go!"

I walked up to the militiamen, who seemed puzzled as they handed me my ID card. "What kind of bribe did you give our boss?" they inquired.

"Nothing!" I replied.

After getting my ID card, the same man who had challenged me as a "man of God" to retrieve it now instructed me, saying, "Go! But . . . ." He never completed the sentence.

I left the roundabout. After walking a few meters downhill, I caught up with my friends, who sat beside the road not knowing whether to continue. They were so discouraged because they thought I had already been killed. Pierre had told them about the last scene he had witnessed as he had tried to bribe the militiamen for my release. They never thought they would see me again. It thrilled and surprised my friends to see me alive and well. Once again, God had performed a series of miracles and encouraged our faith.

7

Held Between a "Demon" and an "Angel"

Do you not know?
  Have you not heard?
The Lord is the everlasting God,
  the Creator of the ends of the earth.
He will not grow tired or weary,
  and his understanding no one can fathom.
He gives strength to the weary
  and increases the power of the weak.
Even youths grow tired and weary,
  and young men stumble and fall;
but those who hope in the Lord
  will renew their strength.
They will soar on wings like eagles;
  they will run and not grow weary,
  they will walk and not be faint.

—Isaiah 40:28–31

After our reunion, Pierre, Paul, Samson, Jules, and I joined our hands together as we praised the Lord for leading us up to that point. Pierre was angry when he saw me holding my ID card, knowing what trouble this had caused before. "Do you still hold that ID? Why don't you throw it away?" he pleaded.

It isn't easy to explain why I held on to such an ID when it labeled me as a candidate for death. But, for me, throwing it away would have meant to lie and say I was Hutu so that the militia would not kill me. I knew that being Tutsi or Hutu meant nothing to God. When I learned about God, I had determined that whatever the cost, I would remain truthful and faithful to Him. Rather than lying and cursing, I was ready to die.

For me, tearing up my ID would mean to take matters into my own hands while attempting to save myself. It would show my lack of trust in God's ability to protect me. I did not want to be presumptuous, but neither did I wish to lie by denying my Tutsi identity. I felt confident that God would not let me down and believed that I was acting in faith rather than presumption.

Looking into Pierre's eyes, I responded, "Do you think my life has been saved because I chose to lie? The God who has saved my life from all those past dangers is still the same God, and He will save me even while I am holding this ID."

Pierre did not want to argue further. Just as he had done when we started our journey, he said, "If you have that faith, then let us keep going."

Even though we had witnessed God's miracles, we knew that more dangers were awaiting us, and we could not move ahead without fear. Again, we gathered to pray behind what looked like a kiosk. We reminded ourselves of how God had delivered us from many dangerous situations. We all knew that we were alive due to God alone and not to chance or human ingenuity. Opening our hearts to God, we joined our hands together in prayer and asked Him to go with us.

As we continued our difficult journey, we came to another group of people who seemed confused and afraid, not knowing whether to proceed to the next roadblock or retreat. From afar we could see that the next roadblock was fearsome. I remember encouraging one young man to come along with us. The roadblocks up ahead terrified him. I did not know how far he had already come, but he seemed desperate. I encouraged him to pray and keep moving, but this did not seem to be an option for him. There was no solution for him at all. As I tried to insist and encourage him, he said, "Do you think I have never prayed before or that if I pray now something will just happen for me?"

After multiple efforts in vain, trying to convince him to trust in God, I did not know what more to tell him. His mind was far beyond my ability to help him understand. Probably one needs to be acquainted with God already if one is to appeal to Him as a friend in times of trial.

Held Between a "Demon" and an "Angel"

As we approached yet another roadblock, our fears intensified. We'd heard stories of how people were being killed and thrown into the Nyabarongo River. This was the river just ahead of us, the river we were planning to cross on our way to Gitarama. When we came to the roadblock, our fears grew even worse. It seemed far more bloody and wicked than any we had seen before.

We saw the dead bodies of men, women, and children lying around us. A group of militiamen was sitting on the left side of the road, watching for Tutsis to kill. We dared not look at the bodies or where the militiamen sat, for fear of being noticed. Though dying inside from terror, we tried to appear as if we didn't care so we would not attract the killers' attention.

Jules, however, became so frightened that he could no longer hide it. He almost fainted from the horrors of the bloodshed. His knees shook so much that he stumbled and almost fell to the ground. Several militiamen took notice and called him to come over to where they were sitting. They arrested Jules at this roadblock.

Though he had a Hutu ID, we did not know what would befall him. Sometimes, the militia would kill someone if they suspected the ID was a forged document. There was nothing we could do, so the rest of us continued on out of fear of also being stopped.

From this point until we crossed the Nyabarongo River to Gitarama, there were no more formal roadblocks. Instead, every inch of the way became a roadblock. The militia had crowded the highway and were inspecting ID cards everywhere. We saw so much killing and chaos. All the phases of our journey had been perilous, but this part seemed the most dangerous.

As we kept walking, I noticed that there were bodies everywhere. Big trucks were being used to carry the dead to places where they were thrown into common graves. Prisoners had been released from the nearby jail to help load the bodies into the trucks.

What I saw was far more than I am able to describe. People were agonizing in their deaths, and even in the trucks people were still moving, half dead. It seemed as if demons had changed into human beings and were now at work destroying humanity.

Despite the chaos, the militia had a well-organized, systematic way of killing. At the place called Nyabugogo, near Kabuga building, a group of militiamen formed a line that blocked the road. Any of the militiamen might ask for

IDs. Hutus and Tutsis alike were being detained and directed to the side of the road. There, someone else would check their IDs and decide whether they should live or die. For organizational purposes, or because most militiamen did not know how to read, they had chosen someone literate for this task.

As I squeezed through the mob, a militiaman grabbed me by the front of my jacket. He directed me toward the side of the road where I would need to show my ID to a half-naked man sitting on a stool. As I was being dragged toward him, I observed that he had a sharp ax with a hammer on the back of it.

The man was sitting among dying people. Some were bleeding and trying to move their heads or other parts of their bodies. He had struck many on the side of the head only once with his ax and left them to die a slow death. About three people were before me, and my turn would come soon. As I saw what was going on, there was no more reasoning about what to do next. But then a prayer came to my mind. "Lord, that man looks ferocious and without pity. If he gets angry, please, Lord, get angry on my behalf!"

The militiaman was still dragging me toward this killer by my jacket, and there were only three or four more steps to go. Suddenly, another hand grabbed me by my collar from behind and pulled me back. I heard him say, "Where are you going?"

"I'm going to show that man my ID card," I replied.

"Come back right now! There is a truck waiting for you back here," he urged.

"No, he cannot go! He must show his ID to that man!" yelled the man who had been dragging me forward.

Meanwhile, other victims were passing me and being killed. After some sharp dispute, the man behind me convinced the militiaman that I would come back that same way once I got into the truck. He said they could check my ID then. The man pulling me back was Jules! He had caught up with us as I was about to be killed by the man with the ax. He was able to persuade the militiaman to release me into his charge right after I had prayed, asking God to intervene! That was certainly God's timely rescue!

I went back a few meters, and sure enough, there was a truck waiting for me. I understood now that God had allowed the militia to detain Jules behind us so that in my time of need, He could use him to answer my prayer. As Jules was coming behind us, he had met someone he knew who had a truck and who would allow us to board together with some other people he had with him. God proved He is God and that there is no other like Him who can answer as soon as His children cry to Him for help.

I jumped into the truck, and we headed toward Gitarama. Many pieces of luggage with people sitting on them overloaded the truck. As soon as I got in, I buried myself under the bags to hide. This helped me pass through the terrible roadblock where I had narrowly escaped death. My sense of security under the luggage lasted only a short while, however, because more serious trials were still ahead. God alone would be my refuge.

The truck was moving, and I was under the luggage bags with people sitting on them and me. It was difficult to bear, and I could hardly breathe. The weight of the bags and the people was too much. But I thought I would be safer there, so I remained that way for a while. My momentary peace was interrupted as we reached another roadblock. As soon as the driver stopped, a man commanded everyone to get out of the truck. I thought I would just remain under the bags, but the man suspected he might find someone there. He shouted in a loud voice, "Is anyone hiding under these bags?"

He started furiously lifting bags, and I knew he would discover me, so I came out and tried to move far behind all the people who had gotten off of the truck. My plan was to linger behind the others as they were showing their IDs to the militia and then come around and mingle with those who had already been checked. I thought the militia might not notice me, but this was not the case. One militiaman was watching all that was going on from a distance. He approached me and asked for my ID. I handed it over to him. As soon as he read the word "Tutsi," he said in a low but terrifying voice. "You must be a Tutsi! You give me money or else I will shout it."

I explained that I had no money and begged for mercy, but he was not willing to leave me alone. Just as he was about to shout, a strange thing happened. Paul, my friend who was standing nearby, (probably also hiding since he did not have an ID) came closer to us. He tried to convince the killer who needed money that if he killed me, he would get nothing.

After being unable to persuade him, Paul stealthily took the militiaman by the hand, turned up his palm, deposited something, and closed the man's fingers around it. At this, the militiaman ran away immediately. He may have been afraid that his colleagues would notice and ask to share in whatever he had received. Later, Paul told me he had concocted a plan to act like he was giving the militiaman money, when in reality he'd just put a simple piece of paper into his hand.

While I was still standing behind others from the truck, the militia found a Tutsi. Their entire focus went to him, and I got back into the truck during the chaos. As the Tutsi cried for mercy, they grabbed him by his arms and legs and threw him alive into a truck full of dead people. Fearing they would kill others, the driver of our truck took off. Later on, the boy they had thrown into the truck of the dead came running up to us as we were struggling to get through yet another roadblock. He told us a policeman had saved him, wondering why he was in the truck full of dead people—still alive and without even being stabbed.

After a whole day of traveling on this horrendous road, we came to an area where there were no roadblocks. We were about to cross the Nyabarongo River that separates Kigali from Gitarama. This was the end of the roadblocks. "Free at last!" We each echoed the words again and again. Crossing this river reminded me of the story of the children of Israel crossing the Red Sea. There was great rejoicing, and we broke into songs of joy and deliverance.

It was still April 15, the same day we had left Kigali. But April 15 was also six days after the militia had attacked us on Saturday, April 9, while we were praying in my house. Across the Nyabarongo River, killings were yet unknown. In this part of the country, life was still normal. We had time to reflect on the miracles that God had done for us. We had crossed our Jordan, passing from death to life. Words could never be enough to describe the joy we felt. Even later that evening, it was impossible to contain our elation. The Almighty God, transcendent and eternal, yet full of all comfort and mercy, this God who had saved us from terrible deaths, had shown His great love for us. We felt satisfied in our hearts!

8

Celebrating Premature Deliverance

If you say, "The LORD is my refuge,"
*   and you make the Most High your dwelling,*
no harm will overtake you,
*   no disaster will come near your tent.*
For he will command his angels concerning you
*   to guard you in all your ways.*

—Psalm 91:9–11

Friday evening, April 15, was very peaceful in contrast to all we had gone through the previous day. Here in Gitarama District, on the other side of the Nyabarongo River, people were still human, and peace still reigned. Only occasional reports of the genocide in Kigali were being circulated.

On our way to Pierre's home, we met one of the militiamen who had come to my house that Saturday in Kigali. I immediately recognized him, and so did my friends. He was part of the group that had looted almost everything I had. I drew close to him, and this time I was not afraid, because he was limping on crutches and had no machete in hand. He also recognized me and seemed eager to get away from us. He feared that we would seek revenge and harm him.

"Why are you on crutches?" I asked. "What happened to you?"

He told us someone had shot him in the thigh in a fierce clash in Kigali in which his attackers had killed many of his friends. He, however, escaped and crossed the Nyabarongo River into Gitarama. My friends and I suspected he was the man who had pounded on our fence door and threatened to burn us in our house. Someone may have shot him while he tried to climb over the fence.

Preaching From the Grave

I saw that the shoes he was wearing were mine. They were the shoes he had taken from me by force. This seemed like a perfect time for getting revenge since he was now vulnerable, but none of us wanted to do that. However, two of my friends insisted that, at least, he give me back my shoes. Though humbled by his injury, his heart had not changed at all. He was not willing to do this. He liked my shoes and pleaded with us to leave him alone.

"Of all the things I looted from Kigali, I have nothing left except these shoes," he explained.

This was nonsense! I tried to convince him to exchange the ones he was wearing for the ones I had on. The ones I wore were older, and I wanted to wear the new ones. But he liked the stolen shoes so much that he kept resisting. He had learned no lessons.

My friends were getting angry and were about to retrieve my shoes by force, but I told them I'd found satisfaction in God and that I did not want to pollute our spiritual climate. I told my friends that the shoes were mine, but we had lost many other things. I reminded them that our lives were more valuable than shoes and that the God who had saved us from death multiple times would also provide for any of our future needs.

My friends agreed with my sentiments, and no one touched the thief. We continued on our way to Pierre's home, where we expected to meet his family. As we traveled, Pierre, who remembered all my troubles in Kigali, tried his best to comfort me. He was planning to help me in Gitarama. He told me to forget about Kigali, because he would help me find a job and make sure I felt comfortable and settled. Pierre was a good friend.

We finally arrived at his home on Saturday afternoon, April 16, tired but glad to be there. His parents, whom I had never met, welcomed us and took me in as their child. We told them of our ordeal. Pierre's parents listened with horror and then praised God that we had made it out of Kigali safely. We ate the first decent meal we had had in days, after which we went to bed and enjoyed a peaceful sleep.

As we woke up on Sunday morning, we remembered that in this rural area, Sunday is normally a day when people bring their tithes and offerings to church or come to perform different chores for the upkeep of the church building. We decided to attend the program and testify about what God had done for us. There was a brief worship service that morning, and we gladly took part. Since Pierre knew a few members in that church, he introduced me

Celebrating Premature Deliverance

to them as an elder in Kigali. Having heard what had happened to us during the previous week, they asked me to share some of my testimony. I agreed and told about several miracles God had performed in our lives.

After the service, the leader of the church asked me to preach to them again the following Saturday. I accepted, and then we went home. For the next two days, I accompanied Pierre, visiting his family members and telling stories about God's miracles in my life.

When we arrived in Ruhango, my friend Jules did not stay with us. He had gone to see his family who lived in Ntongwe, about ten kilometers (six miles) away. On Tuesday morning, Jules came to see us again. His parents had heard what had happened to us and asked him to bring me back to their home so they could care for me. Paul remained with Pierre and his family while I went with Jules to see his parents and relatives. They wanted me to stay with them until we saw if the situation would improve in Kigali.

The kind treatment I received at Pierre's and Jules's homes, along with the love I witnessed from their parents and relatives, was very encouraging. While I had seen how evil the human heart can be, I also saw that good people still existed. I understood that evil had nothing to do with racial differences or one's ethnic background.

The teaching of the media and government that directed Hutus to hate and kill Tutsis had not touched everyone. I knew that God's people came from every group and every ethnicity. Amid chaos and hatred, God still had His people, and He will always have them! I felt at home while with my friends' families.

We were now enjoying peace here and heard about killings happening only in remote areas. We thought the situation would improve. Had I known what was going to happen in a short time, I would have run to Burundi or Congo since the way to those places was still free of militiamen. But I did not know! I could not conceive of the possibility that things would get worse even though the signs were there. Radio broadcasts were still instigating Hutus to turn against their neighbors, even in areas where people had intermingled to a great extent through intermarriages. I was still praying, but God revealed nothing through dreams or visions. As I look back now, I understand that God was in charge. He knew what was about to happen, and He had not lost control.

On Wednesday morning, April 20, there was a midweek prayer meeting in the church near Jules's home. His father arranged for me to preach to their congregation that morning. The large attendance surprised me. I inquired whether this was the norm. They informed me that many had come just to hear me speak, because they had heard parts of my story since Jules had come home from Kigali. Jules had tried to invite as many people as he could for my program. While we had stayed together in Kigali, he had always wanted to invite me to his village, but it had not been possible.

The following day, on Thursday, twenty-four-year-old Claudette and her fifteen-year-old brother, Joel, came to Jules's home. These siblings were seeking refuge after fleeing from the southern part of Ntongwe commune when the militia attacked their village. This alerted Jules's father to the approaching danger. He went around the village trying to collect information. We heard rumors that in the nearby villages, killers were targeting wealthy and educated Hutus along with any Tutsis.

Since Jules and his sister had received a high school education, their father sensed that they were in danger too. Fearing that killers would visit his house in the night, he resolved to find a refuge for all of us. Jules and his sister, along with Claudette, Joel, and I, were in the same situation. The bad news kept coming, and it became apparent that a group of militiamen was closing in on us. Jules and I knew what facing the militia meant. Terror was being revived again.

The newly installed president of the country visited the area, and this triggered the killings in this region. In his speech, while visiting the Butare Prefecture about 130 kilometers (85 miles) south of Kigali, he had stated publicly, in clear terms, that the killing should begin in all corners of the country. He had also clarified that not only should Hutus kill Tutsis, but that those Hutus who were neutral in the conflict should be killed as well. I had heard him speaking on the radio while in Jules's house, and I knew the situation was getting worse.

According to his speech, loyal citizens must kill any Hutu who refused to kill, or was caught hiding, a Tutsi. There was no neutrality. Hutus were being forced to kill Tutsis. Many soon considered anyone of their own tribe who would not cooperate in the killings to be an accomplice who deserved death.

This declaration by the new president was a spiritual challenge to most Hutu Christians. Those who were spiritually weak joined the militia. At first, they did so from fear. Later, realizing how involved they already were, they often became worse than the trained militiamen.

I've concluded that what happened in Rwanda could happen anywhere if conditions were prepared as intentionally and to the same level as they were there. While there can be no justification for the evil that took place in Rwanda, there are several things that may help to explain how people could ever become active participants in genocide.

For anyone to understand how this could happen, one needs to know that those that took part in the Rwandan genocide consisted basically of four groups. Hutu extremists made up the first group. These were loyal to Hutu political parties and steeped in tribalism. They had been taught to hate for decades, and when the time came, they put into practice what was already in their hearts. Though probably few in number, these radicals tried to involve as many people as they could in their determined efforts to eliminate Tutsis.

The second group was made up of hooligans and thieves. These may have been drawn into killing the Tutsis because they wanted to plunder the property of the genocide victims. Leaders of the genocide told these people that when one kills a Tutsi, one also gets what the Tutsi possesses. This group became involved for material gain. As they killed a neighbor, they also rushed to kill his animals and took away everything inside his house. Sometimes, they looted even the roofing sheets. They saw this as an opportunity to enrich themselves.

The third group consisted of those with weak moral characters who were easily deceived. The militia polarized the Hutus against their Tutsi neighbors. In some places in Kigali, the militia and extremist leaders produced forged documents, showing that their Tutsi neighbors were collaborating with the anti-government army. Based on these forged documents, they told the Hutus that it was only a matter of time before Tutsis would kill them. They would have to kill the Tutsis first, before they carried out their killing plans.

The timid and the cowardly made up the fourth group. These would not stand firm against what the government was demanding. There were many who became killers because they feared being killed themselves or called accomplices. Christians turned against fellow Christians who went to the same church. They also betrayed those related to them through intermarriage.

Attempting to justify the killings, so-called Christians would quote Bible examples in the Old Testament when God gave whole groups of people into the hands of their enemies. This soothed their consciences and allowed them to continue praying and going to church, even when all this evil was going on.

If it weren't for God's controlling hand, as He puts in power people of good morals and limits the progress of evil designs, what happened in Rwanda could happen anywhere in the world. When we have peace in our country, we should credit God for our security and peace. We should also make sure we go through the spiritual preparation we need in order for us to stand firm when evil days come upon us. Assuming that we, or anyone else, are on the side of God and will always remain faithful could be a deception.

I saw that there were a few people who remained faithful, like my friends, Pierre and Jules, and their parents. In their times of trouble, they preferred to stand firm, accepting even the risk of death. Though few in number, some faithful souls hid up to a hundred people, using their resources and influence in their communities. After the genocide, the government honored and officially recognized these brave ones as heroes of love toward their neighbors.

What happened in Rwanda taught me that pretending to love God and having a basic knowledge of the truth cannot suffice to keep one faithful in a severe time of trouble. There is a need to hold fast to God now if one hopes to be faithful and not found wanting during the days of trial that can come to anyone. These words of Ellen G. White, which I had read before, became exactly true:

"In every religious crisis, some fall under temptation. The shaking of God blows away multitudes like dry leaves. Prosperity multiplies a mass of professors. Adversity purges them out of the church."[1]

---

1. Ellen G. White, *Testimonies for the Church* (Mountain View, CA: Pacific Press®, 1948), 4:89.

9

Choosing to Die by Guns

"For I know the plans I have for you," declares the Lord,
*"plans to prosper you and not to harm you, plans to give
you hope and a future. Then you will call on me and come
and pray to me, and I will listen to you."*
—Jeremiah 29:11, 12

Peace in Gitarama was short lived. Rumors of killings were becoming a reality. Jules's father realized that he needed to hide us as fast as he could, lest his family become a target. He took the five of us—Joel and Claudette, the brother and sister who had come from Ntongwe seeking refuge, Jules and his sister Jemime, and me—to the home of his friend, Mr. Kalisa, about a kilometer away. But we could stay there for only two or three hours. Mr. Kalisa reported that gangs had targeted and inspected his house throughout the previous day. He reasoned that having us in his home would mean increasing our risk of being found by the killers.

While we waited for what might happen to us, Jules's father searched for another refuge. He contacted his sister's family in another village about five kilometers (three miles) away. We felt anxious and unable to sleep, because we knew that the militia could come at any moment and find us. Mr. Kalisa was also uneasy and feared for his family's fate.

At two o'clock the following morning, Jules's father came back with two men carrying clubs. They were to help us get to his sister's home, where he thought we would be safe. Without wasting more time, we left together, going through the valleys and swamps to avoid encountering any killers. Though there were not as many roadblocks as we'd seen in Kigali, people still patrolled the roads. Some did so for their own security, while others belonged to gangs that were killing and destroying houses in the villages.

Unfortunately, upon our arrival, we realized that this house was already full of many people who had come looking for a place to hide. The small home could not hold all of us. We could stay there for only one day, but we did not know where to go next.

Stories of looting and killing and slaughtering cows that belonged to Tutsis spread everywhere. By evening, the militia knew of our presence. We heard that they planned to raid the village where we were and attack us in the night.

In Ntongwe, up until this time, the militia would not kill the Tutsi spouse of a Hutu man or woman. So, one of the Hutu boys, in whose home we were hiding, suggested that the Tutsi girl, Claudette, should pretend to be his wife. None of us opposed this plan. We then left the girl at this house and went back to Jules's home. We understood that we had left Jules's home in the first place because it was no longer safe to remain there, but we didn't know what else to do.

Upon our arrival, around 1:00 A.M., we learned that educated Hutus were not being targeted. This was good news for Jules and his sister. They did not need to worry anymore. The problem now focused on me and Joel, the boy whose sister had remained at the other house. We continued to feel anxious, because we expected the militia to come and kill us at any moment.

During that night, Jules's father watched in every direction for any approaching danger. Inside the house, his mother cooked food for us. Our presence in their home worried the whole family. They knew people had seen us with them, and that would make their home a likely target of the militia's searches.

Towards dawn, Jules's father entered the home looking troubled. "Where can I hide you?" he asked in a downcast tone. He considered the sorghum plantation down in the valley. For a while, he thought this might be a perfect place to send us. But as he continued to think about it, someone reminded him that the militia had targeted the sorghum field during the day, hunting for people to kill. He then dismissed the idea. There was no hiding place!

Finally, he came up with another idea. He appeared to be in emotional pain. We understood that, as much as he cared for us, he was becoming more and more concerned about his own family's safety. "My sons," he said, "it's better for you to go to Ruhango. Instead of being killed by a machete, the soldiers will shoot you there."

Choosing to Die by Guns

It was painful to hear this coming from the only man whom we thought could be our shield for a while. But I did not have other options, and there was apparently no other way out. I had now reached the point where I was being led like a lamb and lacked the ability to resist.

Seeing me perplexed and disappointed, he added, "My son, I could feed you every day of your life, but there is no place to hide you. You know that when these people come to a home they search everywhere, including the ceiling. And when they see fresh soil, they will dig to determine if someone is hiding in a pit. I don't know what to do for you," he sighed.

"Go. Perhaps a soldier's gun may kill you, which is better than a machete. If they kill you, my son, I am sure we will meet in heaven."

It was almost four o'clock in the morning as we started for Ruhango, about twenty kilometers (twelve miles) away. Jules's father accompanied us that night. He led the way, because he walked faster than we did and was the only one who knew the direction we must travel. He intended to take us halfway to our destination and return home before sunrise. Fearing potential roadblocks, he traveled through the bushes and crossed the swamp in the valley with us following him. The darkness before dawn only made our journey more difficult.

After climbing to the top of one hill, Jules's father stood still and peered through the darkness. He pointed to a hill stretching ahead where we saw lights.

"Do you see those lights over that hill?" he asked.

"Yes," I responded.

"You proceed in that direction. Ruhango, Sous Prefecture is somewhere over there," he whispered.

He advised me not to travel on any road, but to use the fields and cassava plantations to avoid meeting killers on the way. I could see the lights far ahead, but I could not see a thing between them and where we stood. Joel and I felt terrified.

Before leaving us, Jules's father asked us to kneel with him. He understood that there remained no other hope for us. He prayed for us and asked God to forgive our sins so we would meet again on resurrection morning.

Strangely enough, he handed me four thousand Rwandan francs, which is about twenty dollars, before leaving us to continue our terrible journey. This was a lot of money and probably the only money he possessed. I greatly appreciated what he had done for us. He had already taken so many risks on our behalf, and now, out of his limited resources, he had given me all that money. I felt so grateful; I understood that it was all he could do as a human being. He had embraced me as his own son. What love!

After watching him turn and disappear from view, Joel and I continued our difficult journey. We walked in darkness without knowing where to take our next step. Often, we fell into trenches or tumbled down hills, getting up and falling again and again. It was difficult to see anything, because the tall cassava plants engulfed us. We stumbled across fields and gardens, and when we came upon a house, we retreated into the thick bushes for fear of being discovered.

Our confusion intensified as we went forward, and we wondered if we would make it to Ruhango at all. We seemed to be going around in circles, and we kept falling in the dark and hurting ourselves. Sometimes I would be the one to fall, and sometimes it would be Joel. It often took a few minutes for us to get up and regain our composure after the shock of falling. And on top of all these struggles, we realized we were going, not to a safer place, but to a place where we would be killed.

At last, we came upon the main road and decided to continue our journey on it. No sooner had we done this than we met a man carrying a machete and wearing shorts but no shirt. We thought maybe he was on his way to join a group of militiamen at a roadblock. With no way to avoid him, we met directly. After whispering a quick prayer, I said, "Good morning."

"Good morning," he replied.

"Could you show us the way to Ruhango, Sous Prefecture?" I asked.

"Do you think you will pass through this place? Give me your ID card!" he demanded.

I reached into my pocket, pulled out my card, and showed it to him, all the while praying that God would protect us once more.

"You must be Tutsi," he said without reading my ID since it was still dark.

"I'm neither Tutsi nor Hutu," I responded.

"So, you're Burundian?" he asked.

"No," I replied.

"Why don't you give me money, and I will let you pass through before others notice you? But don't give me only a hundred francs!" he cautioned.

Since Jules's father had given me four thousand francs, I carefully pulled

Choosing to Die by Guns

out part of that amount from my pocket. I fished out a thousand-franc bill. I offered him three hundred francs, telling him that he needed to give me back the balance. He agreed, but after showing us the way, he refused to give me back any money.

As we proceeded on our journey, we approached what seemed to be a road-block a short distance ahead. There were many people standing around as if waiting for something. No one spoke. Most of them wore big towels wrapped around their heads or hanging around their necks. It seemed too late to run away, so I went right ahead and met them. I prayed again, "Lord, be with us!"

When we came up to the group of people, I greeted everyone in the group, saying, "Good morning." I moved among them, shaking hands with every-one. Some appeared reluctant, but I moved so swiftly that they did not have time to think. They seemed distant and confused. As I greeted them, I asked, "Are you patrolling?"

None seemed eager to answer, and it was difficult to tell whether it was due to mere reluctance or confusion.

"Goodbye and have a good day!" I said and waved as we continued on our way down the road.

We left them standing puzzled and not reacting at all, armed with their machetes and knives. God had intervened and performed another miracle.

We could begin to see more clearly as the morning hours just before sunrise arrived. I was still cold and kept a towel wrapped around my neck. Because I did not want people to suspect I had slept in the bush or had been traveling at night, I resolved to throw it away and keep moving.

We were now about two kilometers from Ruhango, Sous Prefecture. As we continued our journey walking on the road, we saw a group of women sitting by the roadside. They looked tired and worn out, and I could read fear on their faces. There seemed to be something unusual about them. A woman stood in front of the group, addressing them. As we drew closer, she stopped speaking, and all eyes turned toward us. Although we felt scared at first, our fear lessened when we discovered that they were also afraid of us. They looked so desperate, confused, and agitated.

"Are you Tutsi?" the lady who had been addressing the group asked me.

"Yes!" I answered.

"Where are you going?" she asked.

"To Ruhango, Sous Prefecture," I told her.

Preaching From the Grave

"You will not reach your destination!" she stressed. "They have killed the people who have gone along the way there. Up the road, there is a group of young people slaughtering every Tutsi that comes by."

Her description of the horror ahead weakened us. We became discouraged and uncertain about whether to go on or go back. As I stood absorbed in fearful thoughts, there came the sound of voices shouting in the distance.

"Go behind that house! Go behind that house!" she insisted. "The militia is coming!"

We rushed behind the house. As Joel and I hid there, we heard a group of people talking loudly and others mentioning the name of someone they had not yet killed. They were on their way to hunt him down.

"He doesn't deserve to live!" one among the group shouted.

The lady who still stood beside the road, asked them, "Will you really kill someone?"

"Yes, we will," came the ruthless reply!

She was trying to divert their attention so they would pass by.

After they left, the lady who told us to hide behind the house came and asked us to follow her. We did not know where she was taking us. When we came to a house, she asked us to come in, and we did. She brought us some cassava. This is not a food one can easily eat when feeling nervous. We were hungry and tired, but we could not eat. We could not swallow even a little. Our problem was much greater than hunger.

We highly appreciated her hospitality, generosity, and kindness, although she could see that we were not fully enjoying the food. She asked us where we had come from. We told her we came from Kigali.

"My sons, I wish I could hide you, but I don't know what to do!" she lamented.

"Are you a Christian?" she asked, as she noticed the Bible in my hand.

"Yes, I am. I'm a Seventh-day Adventist," I replied.

"That's my church also!" she said with a cheerful voice.

"Oh, I was supposed to preach in your church today!" I told her. It was the Sabbath on which the elders had asked me to come and preach the previous Sunday morning.

"Forget about that! The church is closed now. No one can go to church," she explained.

She told me that, because the militiamen knew she was an Adventist, they

Choosing to Die by Guns

kept coming to check on her to make sure she was not hiding any Tutsis. She thought that if she tried to hide me, it would only increase my risk of discovery and death. She suggested that we should go back in the direction we had come. After she said some encouraging words to us, I prayed for her, and we left.

Upon leaving the woman's house, we followed her advice and retraced our steps, not knowing for sure where we were going. We realized what we had left behind, and there was no way to continue on that same route. We walked until we found a coffee plantation and hid in it until sunset.

During the day, no militia approached our hiding place. But we could hear them from afar, hunting for Tutsis to kill. When the evening came, we did not wait until nightfall. We headed back to my friend Jules's house again. Since we did not know the way, having come when it was still dark and being unfamiliar with the area, we determined to start back while there was yet a little light, knowing the way would be rough.

10

When Money Could Not Help

Some trust in chariots and some in horses,
*but we trust in the name of the L*ORD *our God.*
—Psalm 20:7

As we headed toward Jules's house, a militiaman with banana leaves around his waist came running toward us. He brandished a bloody machete and looked so fierce.

"You must be Tutsis," he stated.

When we did not respond, he persisted. "Give me money or I'll kill you."

When I heard his demand for money, I remembered that Jules's father had given me four thousand francs. "How much?" I asked.

"Three hundred francs," he replied in an angry tone.

I understood that these people were very poor and looking for money. I felt that three hundred francs would be a good deal. But unfortunately, Jules's father had given me only four thousand-franc notes. I reached into my pocket and pulled out one of the notes and handed it to him while asking him to give me the change. I also told him that he must show us the way to Ntongwe, and I described the home of my friend, Jules, to him.

He did not have change, but promised to give it to me as soon as he found some. He also agreed to escort us all the way to Jules's house. Since he was familiar with the area and knew where the other militiamen were, he could steer us away from any danger. At one point, he ordered us to remain where we were while he went on ahead. Apparently, he knew that there was a road-block and went to check the possibility of us being able to bypass it.

While waiting for him, we thought he might have deceived us. After some time passed, two men, armed with machetes, came in his absence. We knew we were in trouble. They drew closer and leaned forward to see us better under the moonlit sky.

"Power!" I spoke with artificial confidence. This was a slogan for all the militiamen in the region. They used it when greeting each other, to gain other militiamen's attention when they discovered a Tutsi, or to frighten those who were hiding in the bush. Without thinking much about it, I used their slogan to assure them we were not afraid and to ease their tension so we could talk to them.

Deceived by my courage, they assumed I was Hutu and spoke with us. But our peace lasted for only a few seconds. Looking at me, one of the two men studied my features and asked, "Are you not Tutsis?"

"Yes, we are," I replied.

"You will be killed! But if you give us money, we can help you escape. My boss was a Tutsi, and he was a kind man. So, I do not hate Tutsis. But you must give us money."

Suddenly, our conversation was interrupted. The man who had gone to find a safe way for us around the roadblock came running toward us shouting, "No! Those people are mine!"

"If they are yours, give us money, and we will hide them so they won't be killed," one of the men insisted.

A heated argument broke out between them. The two men demanded three hundred francs, and the first man was willing to offer them only a hundred francs. But since he still owed me seven hundred francs, I urged him to give them the amount they asked for so they would hide us. He was unwilling to do this.

After a long exchange of bitter words, the man with my seven hundred francs turned to a nearby tree, raised his machete, and struck a branch in anger. "Do whatever you want!" he said and then ran away, leaving us in the hands of the other two militiamen.

"Please help us!" I begged.

"The only way we'll help you is if you give us money," they stipulated.

I still had two thousand francs remaining in my pocket, so I offered them the three hundred francs they'd asked for. Since I still did not have smaller bills, I gave them a thousand franc note and asked them to give me the difference. They, too, agreed to return my seven hundred francs as soon as they found change.

When Money Could Not Help

"Let's go!" one of them said, motioning to us. "We will try to hide you."

We traveled for a short while until we came to a tiny hut. There was a fire in what looked like one of the two bedrooms, and a woman carrying a baby on her back was cooking some food. We learned that this woman was the wife of one of the two militiamen. They told her to take care of us as they returned to their patrol. The plan they proposed was that they would come back as soon as the way became clear and show us the way to Jules's house. But their intentions were different.

We remained there and continued praying. The woman offered us some cassava bread with meat. Since I was a vegetarian and had decided that none of my life principles would change because of the terrible circumstances in which I found myself, I politely declined. I believed the same God who had provided for all my needs would give me appropriate food at the right time. After Joel had eaten, the woman gave us a mat on which to sleep. Before we lay down, I prayed, thanking God for all His protection and asking Him to take care of us during the challenges ahead.

We'd just gone to sleep when the two men returned and woke us up.

"You must leave right away!" one of the two men shouted. "People are coming to kill you!"

We jumped up and made our way to the door, but when we got outside there were two more men waiting for us—new individuals whom we had not seen before.

"Who is this?" one of the new arrivals asked as he came toward me.

The owner of the house replied, "They are my visitors."

"They are Tutsis!" The other man's tone grew angry.

The new arrivals accused the two militiamen of having hidden us, but this turned out to be a trick. They also asked for money in order to let us go. Knowing that there were 700 francs which the two militiamen still needed to return to me, I asked the man with my money to negotiate a deal with them. But he wasn't willing to give them even one franc. The men who had brought us there forced us to leave their home without giving me my change.

I should have had the remaining thousand-franc note, but now there was no more money in my pocket! I don't know what happened, but it was gone. Aware that there would be no financial benefit in protecting us, the newest militiamen decided to take Joel and me to the nearest roadblock where Tutsis were being slaughtered.

Preaching From the Grave

Unwilling to release us, they led us toward our doom. With no more money to bargain for my release, I turned to God in prayer. I'd thought money could help me make deals with the killers, but I understood now that it was not a big help. God's love and protection were the only real solutions to my problems.

As we walked toward the roadblock, I thought there might be another way to help myself. One of these militiamen was passing by his house and asked the other to take us to the killing place while he went and checked on his home. When he left, an idea came to my mind. I thought this would be the perfect opportunity to negotiate with the man who remained with us. Having realized that these people had few possessions, I started another deal.

"What is it you will get in shedding our blood?" I asked him. I rephrased the question without giving him time to respond. "What benefit do you gain by killing us? Why can't I give you my shoes and jacket, if you let us go?"

He kept silent for some time. Then after a while, he said, "I will accept that."

I stooped down and loosened my shoelaces. I removed my shoes, along with my socks, which were not part of the deal, and handed them over to him with my jacket. He grabbed them from me, wrapped my shoes and socks in the jacket, and hid them in a bush beside the path.

Joel and I proceeded with him a short distance, crossing a stream. Suddenly, we heard a loud shout coming from behind us. We were being followed by more killers. Perhaps when the other militiaman arrived at the roadblock, after checking on his house, and did not see us there, he reported us. The militia must have suspected we had run away. Hearing the shouting behind us, the militiaman accompanying us decided he would go back instead of continuing to help us. He told us that his life was also in danger and that he worried that someone would find his new jacket and shoes.

We ran for a few meters and came upon the main road. It was very stony, making it difficult for me to run. My bare feet were bleeding from several cuts, so I needed to slow down and walk. I thought I'd made a mistake by giving away my socks on impulse when they had not even been asked for.

Soon, it became almost impossible for me to walk, and it seemed better for us to leave the main road. Fearing we would meet more roadblocks ahead, we made our way through the bush. Thorns gouged my feet, and we repeated

When Money Could Not Help

the same difficulties traveling in the dark that we had experienced when we had left Jules's house.

We could hardly see anything, but as I regained a sense of direction, I felt confident we were heading towards Jules's village. When we came out of the valley, we felt exhausted and looked very dirty.

We were about to pause for a rest, believing that no one could see us during the night in that bushy area. But as we came out onto a pathway, we saw two men coming in our direction. They stopped when they noticed us. I thought they were militiamen. It was too late to escape, so we continued on our way toward them. They were supporting themselves with walking sticks. As we walked closer to them, I realized we'd scared them and that they probably thought we might be militiamen. As they turned and ran, I called out, "Stop! Why are you running? I'm not a killer!"

They stopped, turned, and faced us.

"Do not be afraid," I assured them. "Where are you going?"

"Ruhango," they replied.

They explained that they were going there to hide. I told them not to go since we had been going there too and had heard of brutal killings in that area. I also told them not to go to the village from which we had recently come, because they were about to kill us there, and we'd escaped only by God's hand. As I spoke, one of the two men could no longer remain standing. He became so disheartened that he collapsed to the ground and sat before me. In a desperate voice, he said, "We are coming from Ntongwe commune where they have killed seven thousand people. We thought we had escaped, but it's the same wherever we go!" He began sobbing uncontrollably.

I learned that in Ntongwe, government soldiers had gathered Tutsis together, pretending to offer them protection. Then they ordered the militia and Hutu refugees from Burundi to surround the Tutsis and kill all those who tried to escape as the soldiers gunned them down. This was the situation from which these two men had fled.

Their despair touched me, and my heart went out to them. I realized there seemed to be no more hope left for them.

"Can I pray for you?" I asked as I knelt down and held the shoulder of the man who sat on the ground. The second man also came closer as I offered a prayer. "Lord, You have protected these men on the way from Ntongwe to this place. I am sure You can still care for them. You know and see everything that is happening. I ask You, Lord, that their lives may have value in Your sight and that even if they may die, please enable us one day to meet in Your kingdom. Amen."

After the prayer, both men became remarkably strong. "I now understand why God led me this far! It was obviously for this prayer," declared the man who had been sobbing a few minutes earlier. "Even if I die, it doesn't matter," he confessed.

"Be strong. God will be with you," I said.

We bade them farewell as we got up to leave, but they decided they wanted to follow us. I discouraged this idea, explaining that four men going together in the bush would not be the right decision for any of us. They sadly agreed. I remember seeing them leaning on their walking sticks, staring at me as I ran. I never saw them again.

After some time, we arrived at Mr. Kalisa's home—the place we had been hiding when the atrocities started in this area. It was around 4:00 A.M. when we knocked at his door. Mr. Kalisa woke up, worried about what was going on. He could speak only in a low voice.

The militia had terrified him when they checked his house, suspecting he was hiding Tutsis. After we told him what had happened to us since he'd last seen us, he looked even more frightened and pleaded with us to leave. He reminded us he was now the target of the militia, who suspected him and searched his house at least three times a day. Mr. Kalisa was a Hutu Seventh-day Adventist, and the militia targeted their searches on Christians like him.

Understanding our dilemma, however, he hid us at his cassava plantation. As the morning came, I worried that people would see me from afar since I was wearing a white shirt and had given my jacket to the militiaman for our release.

It had started to rain. I thought the rain might solve my problem. I removed my shirt and dipped it in the mud until I believed it would no longer attract the attention of people from afar. Unfortunately, my efforts to tint my shirt proved futile. It was still not dark enough.

That morning, around ten o'clock, we heard a large group of people searching Mr. Kalisa's cassava plantation. They were going across it in a horizontal line, hand in hand, to make sure no one could escape. As they approached where we were hiding, they shouted over and over, "Power! Power! Power!"

When Money Could Not Help

Upon hearing their shouts, I prayed for protection. They were less than ten meters from where we were hiding when something unusual happened.

"Power! Power! Power!" one militiaman shouted as he came close to where I was hiding.

Then every one of them echoed the shout as they ran in another direction. I did not know what had happened, but Mr. Kalisa did. He saw it from his pineapple garden where he was working. The militia had discovered someone who was hiding right next to where we were. They abandoned their search to chase after that person, whom they later killed about a kilometer away from us. We thanked God the group had disappeared. He had worked a miracle for us. We did not realize at the time that our lives had been saved at the cost of someone else losing theirs.

11

Let It Be Wings or Fire

At the time of sacrifice, the prophet Elijah stepped forward and prayed: "Lord, the God of Abraham, Isaac and Israel, let it be known today that you are God in Israel and that I am your servant and have done all these things at your command. Answer me, Lord, answer me, so these people will know that you, Lord, are God, and that you are turning their hearts back again."
Then the fire of the Lord fell and burned up the sacrifice, the wood, the stones and the soil, and also licked up the water in the trench.
—1 Kings 18:36–38

We continued hiding in Mr. Kalisa's cassava plantation until we were sure that the group of militiamen that had been searching there was gone. Concerned that, upon their return, the militia might wish to start where they had left off in their search, we moved to another hiding place. It was just a stone's throw from the cassava field, in a patch of reeds mixed with some tall grass and bushes. We crawled with care, making sure that the grass on our path remained as undisturbed as possible.

When it rained again, we saw this as a mixed blessing. If we changed our hiding place, we could move a little faster, because the wind and rain moved the grass so violently that our movements would not be noticeable. But the bad part was that the rain repeatedly soaked our clothes, and we were freezing.

I had helped Joel to hide in a separate place, about ten meters from where I was hiding. He went into a trench where the grass had grown up and covered the upper edge. The grass underneath was dry, and we removed it to create a space for hiding. I had also done the same for myself further down the same trench.

Preaching From the Grave

Sometime later I heard someone, or something, coming toward me. I held my breath and wondered what would happen next. In that tense moment, I prayed that God would save us again. Suddenly, I could hear a voice whispering outside my bush.

"I cannot bear this. This is death anyway!" It was just Joel. He had risked being seen coming to my hiding place because he was so uncomfortable and discouraged. Ants were crawling on him and entering his ears. In addition, the torrent of water was so great that it started pouring on him, along with mud. He wanted to stay with me. When I tried to convince him to go back, he said he would rather die than go through such a situation again. So, he joined me in my small hiding place. We pressed together and remained there for the rest of the day.

After dark, we decided to leave Mr. Kalisa's place and head for Jules's home. This proved to be a difficult journey. It took over four hours for us to cover a distance of about two kilometers (one and a half miles). We tried to be as careful as possible, making sure that our feet did not make any noise as we walked past houses. We would pause now and then to survey a bush or tree to make sure it was not the outline of some militiaman waiting to kill.

Eventually, we arrived at Jules's home. It must have been around two o'clock in the morning. I knocked on the door. Jules's mother came to open it. As soon as she recognized me, she broke down in tears.

"Where are you coming from?" she inquired.

As I recounted all we had gone through, Jules's father came and listened to our story. They were glad we were still alive, yet they were worried that we had come back, because the militia was conducting ruthless searches. They feared that all of us would be killed.

Further complicating matters was the fact that when I had previously stayed in this home, I had gone to church and preached. Word had spread around the village that Jules had brought a Tutsi preacher from Kigali. Because of this, the militia had been targeting Jules's family and accusing them of hiding a Tutsi. My return would only make things worse for them.

Joel and I were so cold. We wanted to warm ourselves and at least have a change of clothes, since the ones we had on were soaking wet. The atmosphere of the home was quiet, and even the little children spoke only in a whisper. I could see they felt anxious about our presence and had suffered a lot.

They were also worried about me. It seemed as if they counted me as already dead. Jules's mother continued crying, and as I noticed her tears, I could no longer remain quiet. I felt that God wanted me to say something.

"Why are you weeping, mother?" I asked, looking into her eyes with compassion.

"My son, they will kill you!" Jules's mother told me between sobs. "I hate to see them spill your blood," she continued.

"I will not die. God will protect me!" I protested.

"You are just a child and are too young to understand. You don't know what you are talking about. Even Christians are being killed." She then mentioned the names of several church members who were good Christians but had been killed.

One particular case stood out in her mind and fueled her doubts. It concerned the death of a well-known elementary school teacher named Mr. Innocent. Everyone loved him for his kindness and ability to transform unpromising pupils into bright young people who qualified among the few in Rwanda selected for high school. His class had always performed much higher than others in the entire commune. Many parents transferred their children to the school where Mr. Innocent was a teacher, seeking the benefit of his influence.

When killers came to his house, most of them feared to kill him because of his unparalleled moral record. Many were certain that the militia would spare him even though he was a Tutsi.

But things changed. One day, a group of militiamen who knew him well discovered Mr. Innocent hiding and argued about who would be the first to strike him. After some reluctance, one young man stepped forward and did the unthinkable task. Another among the group was disturbed by seeing such an exceptional person killed after all the good he had done in the community. "We have killed many, but God will never forgive the one who killed Mr. Innocent," he lamented.

Mr. Innocent's killer heard this remark, but kept quiet. When the militiamen reported back to their base and recounted what they had accomplished, the teacher's killer informed their leader that someone in their group had condemned him for killing Mr. Innocent, a Tutsi.

"What shall we do with the person who said God will never forgive the killer of Mr. Innocent?" the militiaman asked the leader loud enough so that everyone could hear.

Preaching From the Grave

"Is that person here?" asked the leader.

"Yes," the militiaman responded.

"Finish him!" the leader commanded.

Everybody converged on the boy who had made the sympathetic statement concerning Mr. Innocent. They stabbed him to death. This act had a profound impact upon the group which seemed to sink deeper into brutality. To make things worse, the twin brother of the one whose life they had taken was present. He wanted to run away, because he could not stand to see them murder his own brother, but he was afraid this would only complicate things for him. He stood frozen in fear.

"What about his brother who is standing here among us? Do you think he will support us now? Are we not creating enemies among ourselves?" someone asked, pointing at the twin brother of the victim.

"Kill him also!" the leader instructed.

At that moment, the fate of his dead brother became his fate as well.

For Jules's mother, God was not active in this genocide situation, at least not for now. To her, there was no hiding place and no hope for me. She believed that Satan and evil manipulators were in control of the minds of the people as they ruthlessly killed others.

Hearing her doubtful words, I could no longer contain myself. "I don't worship another person's God. My God, who has protected me from Kigali until now, will still protect me!" I said with conviction.

Realizing my confidence in God's protection, she became quiet. Meanwhile, Jules's father stood lost in thought. At last, he broke his silence. "Where am I going to hide you?" he asked.

He seemed perplexed. He had already sent one of his sons to check around their home to make sure the militia was not coming. After considering many options, he thought of one bush area in Gasuna Village, about a kilometer away.

"Let's try there," he said. "I believe that your God will protect you!"

At about three o'clock in the morning, we started off for Gasuna village. Jules's father led the way through thickets, rifts, and swollen rivers. We felt tired but continued until we came to the bush area he had in mind. The three of us penetrated the heart of the bush and knelt on the wet ground as he prayed for us. After this, he returned to his home, and we remained.

By this time, it seemed we had exhausted all means of deliverance. There was no other place to run to. There was no other home to hide in. Understanding our situation, I resolved to seek God in prayer once more. I asked Joel to keep praying where he was hiding. Jules's father had done all he could, and he had run out of solutions. It was obvious he did not think this bush was much of a solution for us, but there was no other place to go, and we had to leave his home for the safety of his entire family.

We were at the limit of human effort and solutions, but I knew there was a God in heaven. He was in total control of the situation and would intervene when necessary.

Jules's father had risked everything, taking the solitary road with us in the night. At a certain point, he told me he would like to give me his coat since the militiaman had taken mine. It was probably the only coat he had. He would have given it to me, but he reasoned that this would expose his family to danger. In this rural area, most people had only one or two coats, which they wore every day for most occasions. If the militiamen saw me wearing this coat, they would recognize it had belonged to Jules's father. This would confirm their assumption that his family was hiding Tutsis. So instead of his coat, he gave me a piece of heavy sackcloth. This was not much help, because it had rained all night and drenched the sack. It remained dripping and heavy throughout the day, making it difficult to use as a cover.

As I settled into this new hiding place, I prayed to the One I knew I could always turn to. "Lord, You are the Creator of the universe. Nothing is too difficult for You. Whatever is impossible for men is a simple matter for You. Send Your angels to surround this bush and protect us now. Show us once more that You are with Your people. Let others know that You are in control and that You still answer prayers."

My strength was running out, and I struggled to breathe during these terrible hours of the night in the bush! I was almost freezing in my dripping sackcloth, which I had tried to wrap around my body. I kept praying and trusting that God would bring about a solution.

It was around ten or eleven o'clock in the morning when I heard shouting and bells ringing. I looked through the bushes to determine what was going on. I saw a dog moving back and forth as if it were hunting for a wild animal, and I overheard a couple militiamen talking as they approached the bush.

"Would anyone hide here?" one man questioned.

"Even if we did not kill them, the snakes would," the other responded.

Preaching From the Grave

To my dismay, the dog came straight toward me and barked. As I peered through the corner of the sack covering my head, I looked into the dog's eyes as if I were negotiating with the animal. The dog would not move. It continued to make a strange growling noise while staring back at me. I tried to scare it away, but that only made it bark louder.

"You had better surrender," one man commanded me as he signaled his friends, who were already a few meters past where we were hiding. "It's two of them! I have found them!" he exclaimed.

"Come out!" they commanded.

I stood up, holding my sackcloth and the plastic bag that contained my Bible. I made my way toward the militiamen, who were waiting impatiently for me. Joel followed. At that moment, God gave me unimaginable courage. I felt no trace of fear and moved to greet them before anything could happen. Extending my arm, I tried to shake the first killer's hand, but he refused. I held out my hand to the second man, who agreed to shake it but then withdrew his hand right away out of fear. Another man came up and asked for my ID card. I gave it to him. Just as he was studying my ID, we heard a loud bang. Someone was shot about a hundred meters away.

"We will kill you," the man holding my ID card told me.

They then escorted us to the place where they intended to kill us. I felt afraid to die. Most of these militiamen did not have machetes, but knives and clubs with sharp nails in them. I heard them say they called these clubs, *ntampongano*. In the Kinyarwanda language (the language of Rwanda) this means, "There is no ransom for the enemy. There is no bribe you can pay to redeem yourself." By giving their clubs this name, the militia in this area were saying that they were too ruthless to let anyone go.

It terrified me to think of them striking my head with these evil instruments. I tried to negotiate with them and begged them to shoot me rather than kill me with their clubs or stab me to death.

"No!" one of them shouted. "We don't have bullets to waste on you!"

We came to a certain place where some people had gathered. After a quick survey of the grounds near one house, they selected a spot. This is where they told me what to do next.

"Take that hoe and dig your own grave. We don't want to strain ourselves. Dig your grave, and then we will kill you and your friend and bury you both there," a militiaman directed, and the rest of the group shouted their approval.

Let It Be Wings or Fire

Though still weak and tired, I had no option but to pick up the hoe and start digging my grave. I thought about my long journey since the killings had started in Kigali. I recalled all that God had done for me and the miracles I had witnessed. My confident and hopeful prayer was that God would intervene before I finished my grave.

As I dug the hole, the militiamen were bragging about having found us. They were also talking about the horrible way they intended to kill us. Some suggested that they did not have to waste bullets, and others suggested that it was better not to waste their strength in hitting us. I heard one propose that they should just bury us alive.

Though I felt fearful, I also felt that these people were not only doing evil, but that they were like demons, looking down on God as they killed innocent people and made light of what they were doing. I pleaded with God in prayer, asking Him to show Himself as God and to let these killers learn about His power.

"Lord, I have preached about You since my youth. I have talked about the experience of Daniel in the lions' den and shared the story of Shadrach, Meshach, and Abednego in the fiery furnace. I've told people that You worked miracles in ancient times. Are You still the same God I have been serving? If You are the same, show me I have not told lies to others. Show me You are the same God. Do something, Lord! Whatever You choose will be fine with me." Thus, I continued to pray as I dug my grave.

While I was digging, one militiaman picked up my Bible from where I had laid it down. He opened it for amusement. But as he turned the pages, he seemed to show some interest in what he was reading. He became curious about the highlighted sections throughout my Bible.

"What do these colors mean?" he asked. "Why are they different?"

"Those are my favorite verses. They have strengthened me, and that's why I highlighted them," I responded.

The man continued to look through my Bible. As he opened page after page and read every highlighted verse, his interest was increasing. He seemed to have gone beyond mere curiosity to reflecting on what he was reading.

"You mean you have read all these verses?" he asked.

"Yes," I responded, looking up from the ever-deepening hole. I feared that my grave might be finished before God could do something. I continued to pray. This time, I gave God suggestions about how to answer my prayers. "Do something about this, oh Lord! You can send down fire and all of us will run."

I kept praying with an expectation that fire would come from heaven at any moment, and everyone would have to run for his life while Joel and I walked away. But there was no fire. God seemed to be silent.

"You never run out of resources. You can send thunder which will scatter us all!" But God did not send thunder.

"What are You doing about this situation? I will soon finish the grave, and all these people will not learn about Your power! Do something about this now! You can give us wings, and we will fly away before their eyes." Yet there were no wings given as I waited.

Interrupting my flow of prayerful thoughts, the man who was holding my Bible spoke up again. "Brother," he said with sincerity, "before you die, I beg you to give me this Bible."

"That would be fine," I replied. "You may have it."

One militiaman standing toward the back of the crowd objected. "That Bible does not belong to you alone," he told his companion. "It belongs to all of us! If you want it, give us some money!"

"Whatever amount you ask, I will give you," said the man holding my Bible.

I continued digging and praying. But God seemed not to be answering my prayers. I felt impatient, but I knew He was in charge. I kept praying, expecting something to happen!

Moved by what he was reading, the militiaman who was holding my Bible made a request of the group. "I know we will kill these people, but will you please allow me to help him finish digging this grave?" he asked.

Having been touched by the Word, he was trying to be compassionate toward us. He did not want us to continue suffering although he knew they would eventually kill us. But this was not a good solution for me, since the faster the grave was dug, the sooner they would kill us! We needed more time, not less!

The kind militiaman's offer to help pleased the others, who believed that I had been attempting to delay the inevitable. He jumped into the pit and helped me get out so that he could dig.

Knowing he would soon finish the grave, I intensified my prayers. "Lord, this man is very strong, and he will finish the grave now. What are You doing about this situation?" I felt anxious. For me, finishing the grave meant an immediate and torturous death. God was delaying, and I was almost out of time!

Although I thought of the finished grave as the final deadline for God to intervene on our behalf, I discovered that there was something I still needed to learn. God wanted to teach me the lesson that He is always on time, even when He seems to be late! He is always there, even when He seems to be absent. For Him, there is a way out, even when there seems to be no way! I needed to remember that God did not intervene *before* the three Hebrew boys were thrown into the fiery furnace. He also did not intervene *before* Daniel was thrown into the lions' den! All the time I had been suggesting to God what He should do for me, He was already answering my prayers and was only leading me through a process.

As soon as the grave was finished, one militiaman shouted, "No, brothers! This is not the right thing to do! It is not even fair!"

Everybody wondered what had happened and turned their attention to this man as he laid out his complaint. "Why should we bury these strangers in our field? We don't know them. This is private property. Instead, we should let this Tutsi dig another grave along the main road because that is state property. We should use this grave to bury our friend's brother-in-law instead!" He spoke his words with conviction, and everyone agreed with the suggestion.

I later learned that the man they decided to bury in my grave was a Tutsi who had been shot right at the time when they had discovered us hiding in the bush a few minutes earlier. His sister was married to a Hutu. He had tried to hide in the bush, but feared the militia would discover him and kill him with machetes. To make death easier for himself, he asked his brother-in-law to shoot him, rather than face being killed by strangers.

They brought the body of that man, and after they had laid him in the grave, one of them suggested, "Why don't we pray for this man before we bury him?" Then he said, "Mary, mother of Jesus, receive him!" Everyone else in the group just repeated the same prayer: "Mary, mother of Jesus, receive him." Then some men took shovels and filled the grave with soil. They took turns, and in a short time the burial was over.

Hearing their prayer, I wondered what they were doing. I concluded that they were scorning God and acting out of ignorance regarding biblical teachings. How could they kill innocent people and then pray for them? After observing these things, my mind-set shifted. I was no longer thinking about myself and praying for my safety. I forgot about my problem and focused on theirs. Once again, I felt a strange courage coming over me as I prayed,

"Lord, these people don't know You. Help me now. Even if I may die, allow me to say something that will change their lives for the better. Don't let me die before I tell them who You are!"

12

Preaching From the Grave

But you are a chosen people, a royal priesthood, a holy nation,
God's special possession, that you may declare the praises of him
who called you out of darkness into his wonderful light. Once you
were not a people, but now you are the people of God; once you
had not received mercy, but now you have received mercy.

—1 Peter 2:9, 10

After burying the other man, the militiamen led me to the new gravesite they had selected for me. This second gravesite was close to the road, beyond any privately owned property. It made more sense for the militia to bury me there, because that land belonged to the government. Looking over the area, I realized that it provided an ideal setting for preaching! There were smooth rocks and short, green grass where the people could sit and listen to my final sermon.

"Would you please give me my Bible so I may say something before digging another grave?" I asked the man who was holding my Bible.

"Yes, go ahead and teach us," he said.

"No!" protested a man who was standing close to him. "What is he going to teach us? We don't want him to teach us anything! He is our enemy!" His fury was attracting the whole group's attention. "What can he teach us?" he kept insisting.

"We have the right to kill him, but we have no right to refuse to let him talk!" my new "brother" in the militia said in my defense.

In no time, the heated discussion between these two caused a sharp division among the group of over forty people. Some agreed to let me speak, while others opposed the idea. Tension was mounting, some were getting angry, and all of them seemed ready to fight over my case. After some intense debate, one man proposed a solution.

"Hey, why are you guys going to kill each other over someone you don't even know?" he asked. "Let me tell you what to do. Anyone who does not want to listen, sit down and close your ears. Those of you who would like to listen to him, sit down also and listen as he speaks. After that, we will kill him."

This seemed agreeable to everyone and, though they appeared confused, they all sat down. The man holding my Bible handed it to me. I looked for a strategic position—a place where everyone could not only hear my voice but also see me. As I moved forward to speak, I noticed that no one had covered their ears! They were all waiting with great anticipation and listening with full attention.

I was ready to speak, even weak as I was and standing near my new gravesite surrounded by killers holding sharp machetes, guns, and long knives! It was hard to conceive what was going on! I cannot take credit for what happened at this moment. The hand of God was at work, and I believe that He was taking over. I can only summarize what I remember saying. Being filled with power and authority, I began by expressing my gratitude.

"Thank you for your kindness in allowing me to say something before digging another grave." I searched each face and looked straight into their eyes as I spoke. "I want to commend you for praying before burying your dead as you did a few minutes ago." Then I paused before adding, "But you are doing this out of ignorance! There is something you need to know."

At this point it looked like several other people had joined us from the surrounding villages. There were men and women of all ages, along with children. One old man who had been cheering on the young killers was now listening with eager interest. Many had come, driven by curiosity, to see a stranger experience a brutal death.

"It's better to let people pray for themselves before they die, because after they are dead, your prayers have no value to them," I continued. "Let no one tell you he will pray for you after you are dead. It is only now, while you are still alive, that you can pray for yourselves and benefit from the prayers of others. This is the only chance you have to place your life in God's hands."

I opened my Bible, turned to Ecclesiastes 9:5, 6, and read,

Preaching From the Grave

"The living know that they will die,
   but the dead know nothing;
they have no further reward,
   and even their name is forgotten.
Their love, their hate
   and their jealousy have long since vanished;
never again will they have a part
   in anything that happens under the sun."

"I am not pleading for my release. There is no favor I am seeking from you, because I know that even if you kill me, a day is coming when I will rise again. And even now you can do only what God allows you to do," I continued to speak without interruption.

"I want you to understand what is going on. You are fighting a war, the nature of which you know nothing about. This war is not about Hutus against Tutsis, because there are many from both tribes who are not part of this conflict. The real war is between Jesus Christ and Satan. As you know, many innocent people are being killed. The issue is not this current death, for everyone will die someday. The real issue is the eternal death, for it is final. Those who obey God need not fear this present death because when Jesus comes, they will live again. But those that disobey God will perish forever. The second death is the death that all of us should fear. There are many Hutus and Tutsis who will not get involved in this ongoing conflict because they know what is really going on."

I turned my Bible to 1 Peter 2:9 and read, "But you are a chosen people, a royal priesthood, a holy nation, God's special possession, that you may declare the praises of him who called you out of darkness into his wonderful light."

As I commented on this verse, I could see streams of tears falling from many eyes. I saw several people stand up and move behind some big trees as they tried to conceal their tears or talk to one another.

"The chosen ones Peter is talking about here can be found among the people you call Hutus and Tutsis. There are people you are killing right now who no longer place their ethnic identity before their spiritual identity as God's children." With these words, I concluded my short sermon.

I believe there is no way I could have said what I did and be understood the way they understood me that day based on my ability to convince or persuade. It was only by God's power, working through me as a weak instrument, that I could declare this message while I awaited the most horrific moment that can befall a human being.

As I finished speaking, I could see a lot of commotion. The militiamen and others were forming groups of threes and fours, consulting and arguing. There was much agitation and weeping.

From what I was observing, I knew that God had spoken to their hearts and had stirred a change in their feelings. I believed God had given them a chance to make up their minds. They could now decide on whose side to stand in the ongoing conflict. Having nothing more to add, I announced to the group, "I can now dig my grave, and then after I finish, I will say my final prayer."

To my way of thinking, my next prayer and God's answer would be like what happened for Elijah on Mount Carmel. I failed to remember, however, that the Bible does not record two cases like that of Elijah's victory over the prophets of Baal. Neither do we have two cases of a "Daniel in the lions' den" type of deliverance. God has always worked out His will in various ways of His own choosing and in His own perfect timing.

My sermon had lasted about fifteen to twenty minutes. As soon as I announced my willingness to dig another grave, one man who had threatened to brutally kill me cried out to the group, "I know that I instigated all of you to kill this man without mercy, but if any of you kill him, may his blood be on you, not me!"

Upon hearing these words, everybody exclaimed, "Let him go! Let him go! Let him go! Don't let his blood be upon us!"

The leader of the militia stepped forward and asked all the spectators, "Do you agree that we should let him go?"

"Yes!" they shouted in unison.

"We will let him go," he said. "But before we do so, let me caution the women among us, since I know there could be gossiping. If any of you leaks information about us releasing this *inyenzi*,* we will be killed. But before we are killed, we will kill whoever releases this information."

---

* *Inyenzi* (cockroach) was a dehumanizing term used to refer to Tutsis, especially by the Rwandan Patriotic Front soldiers as they sought to create the idea that Tutsis were not human beings.

Preaching From the Grave

"Let him go! Please let him go! We will not talk!" they all shouted.

Realizing the mood within the mob, I asked them if they would allow me to pray for them, and they all consented. I closed my eyes and prayed, "Lord, thank You for showing Yourself to these people today. Your eyes see what is happening now. Thank You for making these people hear and accept Your Word. Please help them understand the nature of the war they are fighting. Help them understand it is not about Hutus and Tutsis but is a war between good and evil. You know these children of Yours well. Please forgive their sins, in Jesus' name, amen."

As I finished praying, the leader of the militia was the only one who spoke. He motioned to two young militiamen, and pointing to Joel and me, he ordered, "Take them to your house and hide them lest other *interahamwe* (militiamen) who did not hear him preaching come and kill them."

The two militiamen picked up their nail-clubs, and we followed them, leaving the speechless crowd behind us. I wish there had been time for follow-up with a further message and explanation of the truth I had introduced. This might have been the only and final message for some of them, which they would need to accept or reject, thus closing forever their eternal destiny. Joel and I marched ahead as we glorified God in our hearts for what had just happened. We did not know, however, that there was still much to suffer and much to learn about God's love and protection.

13

Served by Killers

Then the word of the Lord came to Elijah: "Leave here, turn eastward
and hide in the Kerith Ravine, east of the Jordan. You will drink from
the brook, and I have directed the ravens to supply you with food there."
So he did what the Lord had told him. He went to the Kerith Ravine,
east of the Jordan, and stayed there. The ravens brought him bread
and meat in the morning and bread and meat in the evening, and he
drank from the brook.

—1 Kings 17:2–6

We walked for a distance of about three hundred meters till we came to a
small hut. This was the home of one of the two young men accompanying
us. They gave us some wooden stools on which to sit. After a few minutes,
they fixed cassava bread with some meaty soup for us to eat. I tried to eat
the cassava bread alone, but it was difficult without soup to dip it in. *Ugali*
(cassava) bread is a terrible food if you try to eat it without some good soup!

But I remained firm in my dietary convictions. Though I was hungry,
this was more serious than a food issue. It was a matter of principle. At
moments like these, I often drew inspiration and encouragement from
my favorite Christian author, Ellen G. White. In her book, *Education*, she
wrote, "The greatest want of the world is the want of men—men who will
not be bought or sold, men who in their inmost souls are true and honest,
men who do not fear to call sin by its right name, men whose conscience is
as true to duty as the needle to the pole, men who will stand for the right
though the heavens fall."[1]

When I politely refused to eat the soup they offered me, our hosts, who had learned that I was a Seventh-day Adventist, became curious. "So, Seventh-day Adventists don't eat meat?" one of them asked.

"Some eat it, but others don't. I have decided not to eat it," I responded.

Though they could not fully understand my reasons, they seemed satisfied with my answer. Worried about what I could eat, one of them offered to get me some fresh beans from the field. He then left, promising he would fix a vegetarian meal for me. It took a short time for him to come back with the beans and get them ready for my preferred meal. He also went to a place where bananas were ripening and brought me some fresh bananas.

While I was in this tiny hut, things were not as good as I thought at first. It might be true that some people were sincerely turning to God and were ready to abandon their evil practices after I had spoken to the group beside the road. There had been many tears, and I wanted to believe that there was genuine repentance. But though it was not easy to judge, I observed later that for many, their conversion was not complete.

I felt this was the case for the two young men who had been given the responsibility of caring for Joel and me. They seemed to have realized that God is almighty, and that He has His people among the Tutsis and Hutus. They probably believed that they were fighting the devil's battle and not the Hutus'. But they were still far from fully giving their lives to Jesus.

We had been released and were being cared for, not because they were now turning from evil to living a godly life. They were still killers! But just as God sent bread by ravens to feed Elijah, so these two young men were showing kindness to us without necessarily knowing why they were doing so.

Right after we had finished eating, our protectors received a message from the larger group. Their commander told them not to let us go outside the house, since many people were being killed and more militiamen had arrived who were not present when I preached. He feared we would be in great danger if we were discovered.

After delivering this message to us, the two militiamen told us they were going to join others to hunt Tutsis! They assured me, however, that they were on our side and that we would not be killed. They were planning to dig holes, if need be, to hide us in until the war was over. But this protective attitude was only for us, not for other Tutsis.

This gave me the assurance that God's angels had been present both before and during my sermon to turn the hearts of the killers and impress them with God's power. God was the one in charge, not the people who appeared to have become good momentarily! Of themselves, without God's influence, they would not have had any mercy on us.

We stayed in the house as directed. When the young men returned in the evening, they brought back lots of meat from cows that had once belonged to Tutsis.

A new problem soon arose as we continued to stay in the small hut. There was an elderly lady, a grandmother to one of the young men, who lived with him. She was insane, maybe because of her age. She would often shout or cry. At other times, she would talk loudly, saying strange things. "Who are these people I see here?" she would ask. "Where do they come from and what are they doing in my home?"

I feared she would call attention to our presence in this house and that other militiamen would come and kill us. Worse yet, although the women who had heard me speak had promised not to leak any information concerning our release, rumors of what had happened quickly spread. Our sense of security was short-lived. One of the young men came running frantically into the hut as if someone had found him out.

"Get out of my house!" he demanded.

This was one who had assured us of his protection, but now things had changed. He was different, and I could tell that he feared for his life. I tried to inquire about what had happened, but he paid no attention to my questioning.

"Go out!" he insisted angrily and kept looking over his shoulder.

It was around 11:00 A.M. the day after I had preached. I feared someone would see us. As soon as we left the house, anyone who noticed us would call for the killers. I begged him to wait until evening before making us leave, but he pushed Joel and me out the door.

"They are coming, and they will kill me! The whole village knows you are here. They will kill me if they find you in my house!" he lamented.

I tried to insist that he let us stay inside until nighttime so we could leave when no one would see us. "You go! Your God will protect you," he said with confidence. "I have no God! They will kill me!"

Joel and I had no choice but to leave. We crawled through the bean field, trying to move on our stomachs, making sure we remained as invisible as possible. We hid a few meters from the hut, lying on our backs since lying on our sides would have made us visible above the short bean plants. All the while we prayed for God's protection.

Soon after we had settled into our new hiding place, we heard a large crowd descending upon the young man's house, seeking to verify our presence there, but they did not find us. God had preserved our lives again.

The sun was scorching. Sometimes it felt as though we would not make it until the evening. It was almost too much to bear. We could hear many people moving about and feared they might see us since we were close to the road. We praised God that they could not. From the conversations of those who walked past, we could hear how the genocide was progressing. Some were celebrating their successes in killing Tutsis, while others were announcing their determination to find and kill all the Tutsis they had not yet found.

1. Ellen G. White, *Education* (Mountain View, CA: Pacific Press®, 1952), 57.

14

Amazing Solution for an Unbearable Situation

The L<small>ORD</small> is my shepherd;
I shall not want.
He makes me to lie down in green pastures;
He leads me beside the still waters.
He restores my soul;
He leads me in the paths of righteousness
for His name's sake.

Yea, though I walk through the valley of the shadow of death,
I will fear no evil;
for You are with me;
Your rod and Your staff, they comfort me.
—Psalm 23:1–4, NKJV

After hiding in the bean garden all day until late in the night, Joel and I decided not to go back to the bush where the hunting dog had discovered us. We knew people were wild in this area and that they were already looking for us.

That night, we went back to Jules's house. We knew we had been a burden to his family. Every time they had seen us return, they worried about their own lives. But since Jules was the one friend that we knew in the area, and since his father had shown kindness to us, they were the only people we felt we could count on.

When we arrived at Jules's home, we learned that the news about the grave

Preaching From the Grave

I had dug and the preaching that had taken place had spread all over. When Jules's family heard the reports of our lives being spared after I preached to the killers, they praised God. But they did not know what had happened to us since, because we had been hiding in the militiaman's house. They could not ask many questions of anyone to follow up and check on our welfare because this could have been a risk for them.

We arrived at their home late in the night, probably past midnight. Upon our arrival, there was a lot of joy and praise. I remember Jules's sister saying that since the people of Gasuna village had not killed me, she believed I would take part in the final proclamation of the three angels' messages (see Revelation 14:6–12).

While excited about our arrival, the family also felt anxious again about our presence and the risk this could bring to them. No one could be sure whether the militia had seen us come into their house. This made our stay a short one.

Jules's father felt worn out after all he had been through. He asked two of his sons, Jules and his older brother, Karara, to look for another area of bush where they could take us. He believed, as did I, that our safety had nothing to do with where we were hiding. There was no safe place to hide, and all of his previous efforts to find us a good hiding place had proved futile.

That night, Jules and Karara found another place a short distance from their home. The bush here was thicker than any other we had tried to hide in before. It was also thick enough that someone walking by would not be able to see us without effort.

As we entered this area in the night, thorns and thistles met us. They sometimes scratched our faces and gouged our legs and feet. When we had walked only a few feet into the bush, Jules and his brother prayed for us and left, promising to come and see us the next day.

The morning was approaching. We looked around to find a place where we could lie down. Selecting a spot between some trees, covered by several leafy branches, we decided this was a satisfactory place to make our "beds." We took time to thank God for what He had done for us, and we remained confident He would continue providing for our needs. We did not try to look for a more suitable hiding place. Our efforts to hide earlier had not helped us at all. We knew that anyone who came into the bush there would find us anyway, so we relied on God alone for protection.

Amazing Solution for an Unbearable Situation

As I looked around, I thought I saw something. Sure enough, it was a pair of shoes! As I tried them on, I found that they fit me well. I was excited, recognizing this as a solution for my wounded feet! This excitement did not last though. As I wondered about who could have left the shoes there, it occurred to me that a Tutsi had likely been hunted and fled for his life or had been caught and killed. I felt saddened by the thought of his fate. It reminded me that there was no safety in this place for us.

Still, that poor man's shoes became a blessing to me. I would use these shoes in this thorny bush as I went in and out of the area. Having shoes was important, because every day we would stay in the bush, and every night we would go outside to sleep. Doing this made it easier for my friend, Jules, to come and see us in the night as he had promised to do. I could also use the shoes when I went down in the valley to drink water at around three o'clock every morning.

A few days passed as we followed this routine of lying in the same position with little to no movement. We could still hear people hunting around us. Every time I looked at my shoes, it was a reminder that at any moment the militia could come and find us. I was feeling so tired and disheartened as the dreary days turned into wearisome weeks.

The month of April was rainy. In a way, this was a solution to our problems. The militia could not hunt for their victims when it was raining. But the rain was also intolerable in other ways. Every time it rained, torrents of water would come our way and find us wherever we were.

It was extremely cold inside the bush. Even when there was a little sun, there was no way we could go outside the bush to warm ourselves during the day. The leaves on the trees kept dripping water on us and making our situation worse. It was as if it were always raining. This made our lives miserable and almost impossible to bear.

By this time, my body was shaking, and my muscles had become numb. I was freezing, and my suffering was continuous, all day long. It was as if my body were yelling, "Enough is enough!" Eventually, I developed a cough that persisted day and night.

I remember one time, as I struggled to breathe, Jules had come to see us around midnight, when he thought no militiamen would be on the road. That night, he found me coughing nonstop. He became apprehensive as he heard me struggling to breathe.

Preaching From the Grave

Jules's main concern was not that I was sick. To him, the problem was much more than that. He knew that if the militia at the roadblocks heard someone coughing in the bush at night, they would know it was a Tutsi. He feared they would come and kill us all.

Jules worried about his fate and ours. He had committed to come and see us every night, going through bushes and avoiding the use of the normal path, hoping not to encounter any militiamen. Besides the risk of discovery, Jules could not run if the militia assaulted him. He had an accident in the past which left him almost crippled in one leg and thus very vulnerable. Sitting that night in the bush with us, he said, "Please, please, do something and try not to cough! This is too dangerous for all of us!"

"I will not cough anymore!" I said resolutely.

As soon as I promised, though, I coughed over and over again. Neither Jules nor I had known, as young as we were, that his request was a difficult one and my promise was impossible.

The next morning, I felt so sick. My body was worn out, and my throat was painful. I had reached the point that even food was difficult to swallow due to the sores in my throat. My skin was like a dry leaf in summer.

I wondered why this was happening. God had saved my life, but now life had no meaning at all. It seemed like death would have been better than to have to continue suffering this way. I struggled with negative feelings because of my physical pain. Wasn't God on my side? If yes, then why did I have to endure this terrible life in the bush? When was this going to end? These were questions I was dealing with that were causing me to feel so disheartened.

As I continued thinking about my situation, I resolved that I would either live a life worth living or die and rest at last. An idea came to my mind. Some days back, I had preached to killers, and they had changed their minds once they came to understand God's power. *What if I preached to killers again instead of decaying in this bush?* I pondered.

At last, I determined to develop a controversial sermon and then go face the killers at a roadblock. I would preach the Word of God to them, and God would work a miracle as before and help me be free from this dreadful life in the bush. This is how I reasoned. It would be a kind of power encounter. I did not want to think of the possibility that God might not work a miracle again, but if so, death was preferable to this endless suffering.

That evening, when Jules came, I told him what I had been thinking of

Amazing Solution for an Unbearable Situation

doing. I asked him to help me go to the nearest roadblock so I could face the killers. I explained that life was getting impossible. When he tried to question my decision, I assured him that death would be better than the life I was living at that moment.

After pausing for a while, Jules spoke. He told me I was mistaken and not seeing things clearly, because of the situation I was in. He also said he believed it was not God's will for me to face the ones who we knew were still killing thousands of innocent people. As he described them, it appeared as though the Holy Spirit might have already abandoned these killers.

According to Jules, even if I could convince some of them at one roadblock, I could not convince all the killers in the region. I would have no success in trying to teach them while they were active participants in the genocide. He helped me realize that they were now acting as Satan's instruments. He thought what I was planning to do was like committing suicide.

I am glad now that Jules gave me a clearer perspective of the situation. Because of my suffering, I was trying to force God to work miracles on my behalf. As I thought about it later, after I had changed my mind, I felt as though the devil had been telling me to jump from the top of a tall bridge just because God had promised to help me. After Jules prayed with us, my spirit felt revived, although I was still physically and mentally exhausted.

The next morning, I still felt as weak, tired, and perplexed as the day before. Jules had convinced my mind, but something was still missing. I kept thinking about my situation, knowing that there was no immediate solution. I thought it would be a good thing for me to read the Word of God. My Bible had always been with me, and it had been very helpful. But so far during this genocide, I had not had the chance to read it in the spirit of meditation, taking enough time to listen to what God wanted to teach me.

I decided to seek God in prayer for answers to my questions, rather than going to face the killers. I dedicated my time to reading His Word and praying. Throughout the whole day, whenever I was not reading the Bible, I was praying.

The book of Acts first drew my attention. I believe God directed me to this book for a purpose, because of the situation I was in. I read the whole book through. As I read, I lost sight of what was going on in my life. In every single chapter I found innumerable lessons for me.

When I read the story of Stephen, in Acts 6 and 7, I understood that my case was nothing in comparison to his. Stephen was a man of God who

Preaching From the Grave

testified about Jesus, did wonders and miracles among the people, and saw Jesus standing at the right side of God—yet God allowed evil men to stone him to death.

I was very much inspired by Paul's zeal for the gospel of Christ. He was one of the greatest evangelists the world has ever known and was called by Jesus to preach the gospel to the Gentiles. As I read about his suffering, I somehow forgot my own. One story that touched my heart was the story found in Acts 14:19–20, where Paul was stoned and then thrown out of the city once his attackers thought he was dead.

I felt sensitive to what Paul went through while he was being stoned. His suffering must have been much more than my own! I read that right after being stoned and left for dead, probably with painful wounds all over his body, he did not retreat to Jerusalem to tell what had happened to him. Instead, he went to a city called Derbe to preach the gospel. Luke, the author of Acts, says that Paul went the next day after being stoned! This impressed me so much that I could no longer worry about my own pain. I became focused on who God is, how He dealt with His people in the past, and the surpassing power He gave them to bear all their suffering!

My mind raced through the Bible to other characters that had endured suffering for God's sake. Names like Jeremiah, Elijah, Job, and many others came to mind. The more I contemplated their examples, the more I regained my courage. I felt I, too, could live a life fully devoted to the honor and glory of God.

When I considered the reason for my sufferings, I realized it was not even similar to theirs. If only I had walked with God the way these heroes of faith had, I would have been persecuted for God's Word as they had been. As I considered my life, I realized I had not done all I should have done. Yes, I had preached the gospel, but I had often forgotten the simplest tasks.

I remembered the militiamen who came to kill me in my house in Kigali and who found me reading *The Great Controversy*. These gang members were my neighbors, but I had never taken the time to visit them in their homes to speak with them. I had not done my job as a witness for Christ. I then understood that my suffering as a Christian might have a reason. Maybe I, along with other Christians in Rwanda, had not done our jobs well, but the devil had done his job, and this current situation was the result of his steadfast work.

112

Amazing Solution for an Unbearable Situation

As I continued reading the Bible, I often paused and thought about myself. I could recognize areas of my own imperfections and shortcomings. As simple as they might be, they stood before me clearly, and I felt I would not be worthy to talk to God, were it not for His mercy toward a sinner like me.

It was not only regretful things from my past that I recalled during this time in the bush. The Lord seemed to bring to my mind memories of situations in which He had granted me extended mercy and had protected my life when I should have died. Remembering these things helped give me a sense of the bigger picture of God's perspective and of His purpose in continuing to spare my life.

In the mountainous area I called home, there were physical dangers we faced when it rained. The flash floods and swollen rivers that resulted from heavy rains could easily sweep someone away. As I was growing up, my family warned me of these dangers and told me about the many children who had lost their lives in the rising flood waters. But despite their best warnings and precautions, I had found myself face-to-face with what would have been a watery death had not God intervened.

One day, when I was twelve years old, my niece Anastasie, her friend Asenath, and I needed to cross a bridge made from two trees as we were coming home from school. It had been raining earlier, and we had sought shelter, waiting until the rain dwindled enough for us continue on our way. When it didn't let up, we decided to go home despite the storm. It was almost dark, and the rain was pouring down.

When we reached the small bridge, the two young girls, who were a little older than I, went ahead of me. We could not see one another in the darkness but listened for each other's voices. We were not aware that a raging river now covered the entire bridge.

The water was so fast that it carried along anything in its way. Just one wrong step and one would slip into the torrential waters, to be swept into the valley below. As we tried to move, the two girls managed to cross the bridge. I could hear them saying they were on the other side. I tried to follow in their footsteps, making sure to plant my feet firmly on the bridge. Unfortunately, I could know that my feet were on the right path only when they actually made contact with the bridge. Other than that, there was no way to see.

I tried to move smoothly, walking straight across the bridge for a while, but without realizing it, I made one wrong step. That was enough for what could have been my end.

It took a while for me to realize what was happening. The current was swift, and I was helpless as it carried me down into the valley. I knew I had slipped into the river, but I did not have time to think or cry for help. It was as if I were in a dream, and I had absolutely no control over what was happening. I was flailing as I moved along with rocks and pieces of wood like just another part of the flowing current—the latest victim of a torrential flood, doomed to die.

When my niece and her friend no longer heard me talking, they knew I was gone. It was too much for these little girls to bear! Doubling over in grief, they cried in the darkness.

After being carried about one hundred meters (328 feet) by the raging river, I felt my body hit something! There was a big tree planted at the river side. As I bumped into the tree, it threw me onto the other side of the river, and I was able to get out of the water. I began walking up the valley toward the cries of my niece and her friend. With a weak voice, I called to my niece, trying to comfort her, but she could not hear me over the torrential rains and surging waters.

When at last they heard my footsteps, they stopped their crying, thinking I was a wild animal. As I approached them, they could not believe their eyes until I talked with them and assured them that God had just miraculously saved my life!

I came to them tired, beaten up, and injured by the floodwater debris, but I could feel only amazement for how God had rescued me from certain death. I did not realize I had sustained several severe injuries until the next day at home.

At that young age, I did not take time to think about why God had saved my life and what future purpose He might have for me. But now, lying down and hiding in the bush, there was plenty of time to contemplate these things.

I also recalled a time of divine intervention involving a bicycle which a friend asked me to take to his home one day after church. I had my Bible and was riding the bicycle to his home when I came to a junction in the road. A car was coming from the opposite direction. I entered the junction, because I thought I had the right of way, but the car kept coming too! I quickly stopped, but as I did so, the car stopped as well. Then I moved again, and

Amazing Solution for an Unbearable Situation

so did the car at the same time. I felt that if I kept moving, the driver would stop. Well, he must have felt the same way, because we both kept going until we collided.

The car ran over the bicycle, crushing it. I jumped over the car before impact and landed upright on the other side with bare feet! My Bible had flown off the bike, and I did not know the whereabouts of my shoes. People came running over to the car. The driver had closed his eyes, because he thought he had just killed somebody.

I walked back to the car and looked at the people inside through the broken windshield. I was worried that someone might be injured. While standing there, I heard a person in the crowd that had gathered exclaim, "This was a terrible accident!"

"They hit someone," another person said.

"Where is the one who was hit?" several people were asking, as they looked around.

Everyone, including the driver, was looking for the missing person who had been riding the bicycle. Finally, somebody next to me saw that I had no shoes on. I was still wondering what had happened, where my Bible could be, and about the state of the bicycle.

"Are you not the one hit by the car?" he inquired.

"Yes, but I have nothing wrong with me. I am concerned only about the bicycle!" I responded.

Everyone was amazed that I appeared to be unharmed. They suspected I had sustained internal injuries though and thought it would be a good idea to take me to the hospital for an examination. I tried to refuse, but they forced me to go. When the doctor saw me smiling and acting normal, he did not feel the need to examine me.

As I looked back on these experiences and others in my past, I began to understand that when God has something to do with one's life, it does not matter what struggles one may experience. God can always make a way out of life-threatening circumstances. God had protected me in the past and was protecting me now for a purpose.

All this had caused me to forget about my suffering and my life in the bush. My focus was now on God, His work, and what He wanted me to do. There was no time to think of my troubles anymore during the entire day as I meditated upon God's Word. In my mind and heart, God was sovereign, and I was just a sinner in need of grace, ready to serve Him and go wherever He was leading me.

I praised God as I asked for forgiveness. How could I have ever become so discouraged? I poured out my heart in prayer saying, "Lord, You know the reason I'm here in the bush. I now feel convinced that You have a purpose for me. Let me not consider my suffering anymore. Please strengthen my aching body and help me to be patient until You reveal what You would have me do. Help me see beyond my current situation and make me like clay in the potter's hand. After my sufferings, allow me to do what You want me to do for You."

15

Ready to Die for a Friend

"These are the words of him who is the First and the Last, who died
and came to life again. . . . Do not be afraid of what you are about
to suffer. I tell you, the devil will put some of you in prison to test you,
and you will suffer persecution for ten days. Be faithful, even to the
point of death, and I will give you life as your victor's crown."
—Revelation 2:8–10

That Saturday night when Jules came, I was a changed man. I felt so peaceful despite my increasing physical suffering. When I saw him, I was eager to share my experience with him. I had made a discovery. Not only had I discovered who the Lord was but also who I was. My inner struggle had ended when I surrendered my will and life to God. I felt forgiven and ready to start a new life, beaming with confidence.

Jules looked very downhearted that night. As I spoke, he could only sigh from time to time. I knew something was wrong. Having known Jules for years, I could guess he had bad news to tell me. The last time we had a similar experience was when we were in Kigali and the militiamen had said they would kill me the next morning. Then, he had not wanted to share this information with me, and I guessed there was also a serious problem this time. After much persuasion, he at last told me that things were getting worse.

"You cannot hide in this bush anymore," he said.

"Why? What has happened?" I inquired.

Jules told me about a recent meeting the militia had held. They had decided that they needed to make sure no Tutsi could hide anymore. They directed everyone in the village to search each neighboring bush and keep their own fields free of any Tutsis who might wish to hide there. If the militia found a Tutsi hiding on anyone's property, they would kill that person along with his whole family.

Jules told me how his mother had not been able to sleep for several nights, because she feared that the killers would one day discover that I was hiding in the bush close to their house. If they found me, they would come to kill all her children, her husband, and her. She had attempted to convince her husband to tell me to leave the bush. After much discussion, Jules's parents tried to make him understand that it made no sense to risk the lives of their entire family for an individual who would eventually be killed.

As he explained the situation, I understood the issue was serious. I had appreciated so much all the things Jules and his family had done for me. They had gone through a lot to do what they could to help me. This was something they didn't have to do. They had tried their best to protect me, to hide me from house to house and from bush to bush. Jules's parents had given me food and were daily risking the life of their son, who came every night, braving the rain and the possibility of meeting killers, to bring me and Joel food in our hiding place.

I reasoned that I should not ask for anything beyond what seemed possible from a human perspective. Why would a parent do something when it would endanger his or her children? Many people had died at the hands of their neighbors who had turned brutal. I decided that there was no need for Jules and his family to risk being killed because of me.

Though the last few days in our hiding place had been relatively safe, that did not mean that the war was over. I realized that no one had any solution to our dilemma. Only God could solve this problem for us.

After speaking with Jules, I understood why he was so worried. There was no other bush we could hide in. His parents had given him a week to find another bush in which to hide Joel and me. Jules was in a dilemma. Would he prize our friendship above the lives of his own family? Was he now going to bid us farewell? When he explained what had happened and told me that there was no other bush in which we could hide, I froze in silence. I had nothing to say.

Leaving this bush, which had become our home, meant facing the militia. To complicate things, my body was becoming weaker, and I was still sick. I could hardly walk, and I was still feeling pain in my throat, which made it difficult for me to talk well. What, then, were we going to do?

I wondered if Jules had become too discouraged. Was he now prepared to let us go our way and die? Although I longed to continue relying on his protection and acts of mercy, I felt it was unfair for me to expect him to alienate himself from his family because of me and Joel.

"Jules, I know you have done all you could to help me," I said. "What do you make of my situation? Is this our last moment together? Are you also going to abandon us?" I asked him.

I realized that I was posing difficult questions to him. But in my bewilderment, not knowing what to do or where to go, I felt I needed to know his position concerning our destiny. He had always been a friend in good and in bad times. This must have been the most trying time. I looked expectantly into his eyes as I waited for his response.

"Your death will be mine, and wherever you go, I will go too," Jules spoke with agony in his voice. "I will not abandon you! I will try to find another solution. Even if it means risking my life, I am ready to die with you."

One can hardly imagine the peace that flooded my heart at hearing these words from such a committed friend. There was still somebody in this world with whom I could share my sorrow! It cheered me to know that in Jules I had a true friend, one who was even ready to die for me. I felt very much strengthened.

"There is a God in heaven who cares about us and knows everything, from the beginning to the end," I pointed out. "He loves us, and nothing can happen to us without His permission. Let's tell Him about our troubles and give Him the week your parents have given us for a deadline to leave this place, so He may answer our prayer. Since none of us can find an alternative hiding place or a solution to this problem, we must trust in Him who is able to help us."

I then asked Jules to pray and fast for a week, from that Saturday until the following Saturday. I would have no struggle with fasting because there was no food in the bush. We prayed together, and then he went back to his home.

During the week that followed, seldom a minute passed without me either praying or reading part of God's Word. Since the Bible would be free for use while I was praying, I also asked Joel, my companion in suffering, to read God's Word whenever I was not reading it and to pray whenever I was reading the Bible. I thanked the Lord for His willingness to listen to my prayers. Every verse I read seemed to generate another positive perspective on my situation. My confidence in God was unassailable.

I expressed to God how thankful I was that He had shown me His hand all the way from Kigali until now. I praised Him for having protected us in the bush where we were at that time. In my prayers, I remember telling God that I did not understand why He loved me the way He did. I opened my heart to Him and said, "Lord, You know that I can no longer stay in this bush. You know that I have no other place to go. Nobody can receive me in his or her home without putting themselves in danger. I'm now like a hunted animal. The only place I can go is to You. I have no home. Look! Even the bush You have given me during my suffering is being taken away, and I have to leave in one week's time. Lord, I come to You. Please provide an answer to my problem. This one week they have given me, I also give it to You so You may do another miracle. At the end of this week, show them that I am Your servant and You are my God. You know that I have faith in You, but if my faith is weak in Your sight, Lord, I ask that You may increase it so that my prayers will be acceptable to You. Give me the faith I need so You may answer my prayers."

During that entire week, I prayed, negotiating with God and reminding Him of the times I used to preach every Wednesday before the genocide broke out. I drew God's attention to the many evangelistic efforts I had conducted. I said, "Lord, You know I have trusted in You. I believe that Your promises are all true, and I am convinced that if we pray in faith, You always answer. Now it is time for You to intervene and prove Your love for me. Show them You are a God who doesn't change."

I asked God to allow me, before I left the area, to thank the family that had hidden me for all this time. It seemed appropriate to remind each of them, even those who had doubted, to continue trusting in God's ability to protect His people, even when things seem hopeless. I wanted to affirm that God is always in control of all the affairs of the world, and that He does whatever is necessary to protect His people until the end.

Being in the bush day after day and night after night, I had lost track of what day of the week it was. So, it was not surprising that when Thursday evening arrived, I thought it was already Friday. I was waiting for the end of the week with great anticipation, because Saturday evening was the deadline I had given God to take me out of the bush. I knelt and worshiped the Lord, confident this was the second to last evening I was to spend in the bush

Ready to Die for a Friend

before God would deliver me. Although I did not know how He would do it, I trusted that He was going to do something remarkable. I believed the Lord had already accepted my week-long prayers.

At last, I stopped asking God for anything. Instead, I poured out my heart in thanksgiving to Him in advance for the anticipated deliverance. The following day, I felt convinced that it was Saturday, the end of the critical week of fasting. The day came and passed, but nothing happened.

I was wondering how God would deliver me from this life in the bush. Was He going to give me wings and help me fly out of the country, or was He going to use other means? Every time I thought of escaping by God's providence, I kept praying that God would not allow me to go without saying thanks to Jules and his family.

Somehow, when evening came, I felt a flow of strength. My heart rejoiced, and my hope revived, because I thought something great would happen before sunset. However, when sunset came and night approached, I was so disappointed and confused. I tried to stay optimistic. I continued praying while waiting for my friend Jules to arrive on what I believed was the last day of our week of prayer and fasting.

When Jules came that night, I asked him about any news.

"Has God answered our prayers?" I inquired.

"Not yet," he responded. "But let us keep on praying."

I felt very discouraged. I wondered if God had chosen not to answer. Did I not have the faith I needed? But I had prayed that God would consider that need and give me the faith I lacked! Was there anything wrong in the way I had prayed? What could this imply about my Christian life? Why did God not fulfill His promises?

Realizing something was wrong with me, Jules asked,

"Why are you so discouraged? We still have one more day to go! Let's keep praying for God's answer!"

"Did we not start to pray on Saturday, and isn't today Saturday?" I asked him.

"No, today is Friday! Tomorrow will be the Sabbath!" he exclaimed, amazed by my confusion.

The miscalculation was my fault. Joel and I had no contact with the outside world, and we had lost count of the days. It relieved me to find out I had been wrong. I tried not to fret over the mistake, since I had used the time well. I had spent the day in prayer and preparation for ending my bush life. When Jules came that Friday night and requested me to keep on praying, I felt encouraged once more.

We had been praying for God's Sabbath blessings since Thursday evening. We celebrated God's creation in our talk and thoughts. Now we had one more thing to celebrate! I thanked the Lord with joy upon learning we still had an extra day until Saturday and that deliverance was yet to come. I still had time to rededicate my life to God before leaving the bush.

After Jules had helped me regain a sense of time, I felt so happy it was as if I had already been delivered. I praised the Lord, and from that time onward, I kept on praying. The miracle I was expecting to happen should happen on Saturday, I reasoned. Henceforth, I thanked the Lord, because I was sure He would answer my prayers by sunset the following day. As the Sabbath day unfolded, I was expecting that something miraculous would happen at any minute. Whatever it was, I'd be ready to accept it.

I watched the sun sink into the west that day as I sat hoping intently that something dramatic would happen. But soon the sun disappeared with no miracle occurring.

Joel and I knelt and prayed together. Words were few. I knew we had done all we could. We had expressed our faith in God. I asked the Lord to help me accept His will for my life. There was no more fear, as I prayed for God to show me what I was to do next.

16

Deliverance From the Bush Life

*I will extol the L*ORD *at all times;*
  his praise will always be on my lips.
*I will glory in the L*ORD*;*
  let the afflicted hear and rejoice.
*Glorify the L*ORD *with me;*
  let us exalt his name together.

*I sought the L*ORD*, and he answered me;*
  he delivered me from all my fears.
Those who look to him are radiant;
  their faces are never covered with shame.

—Psalm 34:1–6

It was Saturday, May 28, the day we had expected God to perform a miracle to deliver us or find us another place to go. Joel and I had just finished our prayer session when it started raining. We had planned to wait for Jules to come to us, but we had had enough of bush life. The rain strengthened our decision to leave this miserable existence.

While in suspense, waiting and wondering what God would do as an answer to our prayers, I remembered the case of the four leprous men who had trusted what the prophet Elisha had said. They left their dire circumstances and dared to enter the camp of the Syrians, where they found that their enemies had disappeared (see 2 Kings 7). We resolved that we did not need to see evidence of God's answers with our own eyes in order for us to move forward in faith.

Preaching From the Grave

It was time to end our thirty-four days of bush life. We knelt, and I prayed, "Lord, You are a God who promises and fulfills what You promise. We have talked to You during this entire week, and we are sure You have heard our prayers. We wait for Your answer, but we don't want to stay in this rain any longer. From here on, we will not go to any other bush or hiding place again. Show us the way we need to take. Amen."

I told Joel to follow me. Though I tried to run as much as I could, it was difficult because I felt very weak. I was ready to face whatever the world outside was about to give. We arrived at Mr. Kalisa's home, but decided not to knock. Instead, we made ourselves comfortable under the veranda of his house. It was dark, and no one could easily see us. I prayed for God's protection.

A short time after we arrived, I saw somebody with an umbrella cautiously approach Mr. Kalisa's home. I feared that he might be a militiaman. Since it was dark, the individual could not see us, and we remained out of his sight. After the man announced his presence, Mr. Kalisa opened the door for him. I recognized from his voice that it was Jules's father. I could overhear their conversation from where we were; they did not suspect that anyone was listening and did not speak in hushed tones.

"Are you still here?" Jules's father asked Mr. Kalisa.

"Is something going on?" Mr. Kalisa asked.

"People have left their homes to escape," Jules's father said. "My family and I have also fled. The Rwandan Patriotic Front is approaching."

I could not believe what I heard. Could this be God's answer to my prayers?

Unable to contain my excitement, I approached Jules's father, who was still standing at the door talking to Mr. Kalisa. These two men had shown great kindness to us. Mr. Kalisa had also brought us some food when we were hiding closer to his house. Jules had told me that Mr. Kalisa's wife had become ill and died, leaving an infant behind. He was now caring for the baby.

As soon as Jules's father saw me, he whispered with emotion in his voice, "My son, are you still alive? Your God has been victorious!"

He told me that everybody had fled because of the news that the army was now in the area. "Your friend, Jules, is at home. He didn't flee with us," he continued. "He stayed behind with some children. He chose to stay at home because he says there is no better refuge than God, and he does not want to run away from the killers. Go join your friend. I know that the God you worship will be with you."

Deliverance From the Bush Life

After being told that Jules had remained at home, I went to see him. Before going, I prayed and asked the Lord to give me two signs to show He was the One still directing all the events in my life. I told Him that if He was still leading me, He should not let me meet anyone along the way to Jules's home and that I should go straight into the kitchen, where I would meet only one person. If God would make things happen this way, I would take these as signs proving He was still with me.

On the way, I met no one. When I reached Jules's home, I went straight to the kitchen and found one child seated near the fire. God had answered my prayer by granting me the signs I had requested. When the boy in the kitchen saw me, he became afraid and tried to run away. I assured him that all was well.

As soon as Jules came into the kitchen, he cried indescribable tears of joy when he saw me warming myself by the fire! It was exactly the same time that we had started our prayers a week earlier, asking God to work a miracle. The week Jules's parents had given him to get us out of the bush near their home was the week we had given to God for Him to deliver us. This was no chance, no coincidence! God had answered our prayers!

I stayed at Jules's home from that time on. Joel had come with me, but after a few days, he left to join his sister, Claudette, in the home where she was staying.

My health improved. I could eat and sleep. There were no more mosquitoes as there had been out in the bush! However, I was told to never go outside the house during the day, because the militia was still roaming the neighborhood and could come and kill me. Once in a while, I could hear people speaking outside the house, but I could never stand up to see who they were. I had to spend the whole day lying down. Only during the evening could I get up to stretch.

I was glad to be in a house after such a long time living in the bush. I spent some time remembering all that I had gone through. To make sure I would not forget what God had done for me, I wrote down all the events and dates. I also reminded myself of my vows to God.

Within a few days, we heard that the entire region was under the control of the *Inkotanyi* Army (Rwandan Patriotic Front). We heard they were rescuing Tutsi survivors while hunting down the militia responsible for the killings. We had yet to see any soldiers in our vicinity. It was our belief that the militia was still out there. We'd heard that most of them had fled and that others had come back to take their valuables. There was so much confusion. We wondered if the end of the war was near.

As I felt more confident that the situation was improving, I went outside to stretch and bask in the sun. I was glad I could eat again; however, my body was so malnourished that it could not process food well. Because of this, I developed a condition that caused my legs to swell.

Jules checked with neighbors to find out what was happening, and he learned that the army had ordered people to leave their homes and gather in a certain place. For about a week, word spread that everyone was being asked to leave their homes for designated places of safety. I could not join the others because of my swollen legs, so I stayed in the house, hoping that I would soon recover. Meanwhile, unknown to us, anyone who refused to comply with the order to gather would be considered an enemy by the RPF. Those who had taken part in the genocide ran away, fearing that people would identify them at the gathering. We did not know our security depended on obeying this military order.

Jules was informing the few Tutsis that he knew were still in hiding that the RPF army had come. Day after day, he would go searching for survivors, bringing them from their hiding places and accompanying them to the place the soldiers had designated for the people to assemble. From Jules's home, I could see people streaming along the road, carrying their belongings on their heads. This went on for several days.

One day, I asked Jules's brother to accompany me on a walk since I was still very weak. This time the road looked empty. It seemed like everybody had left. As we walked, however, we came to a place where we caught sight of a multitude, numbering thousands, walking in single file. Everyone was carrying his own luggage, including former businessmen and government officials who were forced to walk like common citizens.

Some later remarked that this was a deliberate attempt to teach the Rwandans that they were all equal, that no one was superior to another. The ground had been leveled. The rich and the poor, the educated and uneducated, the Hutus and a few Tutsi survivors were all walking together as one group of people. Those that were too sick to walk were being pushed in wheelbarrows.

Seeing the mass exodus, we realized that we had neglected to obey an order

Deliverance From the Bush Life

that could mean the difference between life and death. We then decided to go back to Jules's home, pick up our belongings, and join the group. Jules's brother recommended that we use an alternative road to avoid any danger. We had walked less than two kilometers (over one mile) when Jules's brother told me he had seen a soldier. He told me to run and follow him, but I couldn't.

He ran only a short distance when one of the RPF soldiers spotted us and ran toward us with his gun drawn. I thought it would be the end of my life. I put my hands up. With only a moment to pray, my heart cried out, "Lord, save me!"

God answered my prayer. Instead of shooting me right then, the soldier captured me alive, because he thought I was a militiaman who had refused to follow the order to go with everyone else.

"You will die!" he shouted.

I showed him my Tutsi ID card, the same one that had gotten me in trouble with the Hutu militia multiple times. He refused to believe that I was Tutsi, saying that his superiors would not accept that I was a Tutsi either. He wondered how I could be a Tutsi and still be alive there. Even if I were a Tutsi, I must have been a sympathizer with the militia, because there was no reason I should not have gone with the others to the place designated for safety. I begged him to let me go, but he told me it was not possible. Meanwhile, Jules's brother had disappeared.

As he took me to his commander, the soldier advised me to tell any lies that might help ensure my release, but I refused. I prayed instead. I asked the Lord to be with me and to let His will be done. When we came to where the commander was, he ordered me to sit down. I could tell that something was distracting him. His attention seemed focused on a bottle of beer that my captor had in his possession. I sat there, forgotten. After a long time, the commander turned to me with fury in his eyes.

"Who are you?" he asked. "How did you get here?"

I pulled out my ID card and handed it over to him. I told him I was going to the home of the family that had hidden me. The commander still seemed distracted by the bottle of beer. The soldier who had captured me was in trouble, because he was in possession of alcohol while on duty. Sometimes the officer's attention would be on me, and sometimes it would be on the soldier who had brought me to him. I heard the soldier trying to justify himself by saying it was just water in the bottle, but when asked to pour it out, he would not. This proved that it was alcohol. The two of us were now in the same situation, fearing what would befall us.

Turning in my direction again, the commander slapped me on my right cheek. I felt the pain, but it was nothing compared to what I had expected. He told me to go at once to the nearest camp. I obeyed right away and went there.

In the camp, I met many Christians who had known me as a preacher. I was glad to meet Jules and his brother among those who had arrived earlier. My friend, Paul, was there too. We were overjoyed and, for a moment, we forgot about all our suffering.

After everyone was gathered in one place, we were all given instructions to move. Some believed that a new war would break out between the RPF army and the French government troops, who had been displaced in the western part of the country. The RPF told us to move toward a safer area, because they feared attack. I felt this was ideal, whether or not there was a possibility of war. Moving together created in us a sense of sameness as human beings and a feeling of unity. We walked, paused, and stayed together—Hutus and Tutsis without distinction. We thanked God as we celebrated His salvation.

Some resisted the order to move. Along with other survivors, I still struggled with weakness and did not feel ready to move. All I needed right then was to be in a place where I could receive treatment and sleep. I had to use a walking stick, because I could not walk on my own. Hutus who had no physical problems also wanted to stay in their comfortable homes. The order to move was a great inconvenience to everyone.

As we moved, we would pause after some kilometers to stay in a house vacated by those who were also moving ahead of us or who had run away into neighboring countries. We thus explored Rwanda, moving toward the eastern province. In other parts of the country, people moved from cities to rural areas and vice versa.

One thing that struck my mind and touched my heart was that God continued to be worshiped among the people. While traveling without a destination, we were granted permission by the authorities to congregate in the camp for church every Saturday. We discovered that there were so many Christians among us. Some were pastors, and others were church elders or deacons of their respective churches. This made it easy for us to organize well-structured worship services under the trees. This happened in the camps all around the country. These were precious times of fellowship and unity.

Deliverance From the Bush Life

There was no distinction anymore of being rich or poor. No one had a home of his own. We could stay in a house for a day, or sometimes a week, just as we needed, but always ready to continue to the next location when commanded to do so. For a whole month, in this war situation, there were no jobs and no trading, just staying in one place for a little while and then moving again. Everyone was doing the same.

The most important lesson we learned during this time was that we do not have a permanent residence on this earth. Hutus had claimed that Tutsis were foreigners and killed them to possess their lands and property. Now, following the order of the conquerors, we were all moving as wanderers, camping for a while as ordered, and continuing on the next day without knowing where we would stop or if we would ever return.

Later, I learned that the situation was similar throughout the entire country. As a friend of mine told me later, we were being taught that we were all Rwandans and that no one was superior to the other.

The situation seemed to me like the one described in the Scriptures when it indicates that all of us are but pilgrims and live in countries that are not our own (see 1 Chronicles 29:15). We are journeying through this life on our way to eternity. This world is not our home, and we must let nothing divert our minds from focusing on the far better heavenly home where we are heading (see Hebrews 11:13–16).

While many of us were wandering the country, heading eastward, another group of about two million Hutu Rwandans was going in the opposite direction. These were mostly militiamen with their families and supporters. Fearful, innocent Hutus also followed them, because of rumors spread by militiamen that the RPF would kill them in revenge. Among these, were government and military officials, educated and non-educated, rich and poor alike.

There were people in that group who called themselves Christians and people from other religions. These were the ones who had believed that Tutsis were damned to perish and so had condoned and even taken part in the genocide. Religious leaders among them had taught that God had given the Tutsis into their hands to be killed, just as He had commanded Israel to kill their enemies in the Old Testament. But now, they were the ones running for their lives. They moved from one camp to another without knowing their destination until they entered neighboring countries. Living in overcrowded and filthy refugee camps, thousands died from terrible epidemics such as cholera and dysentery.

The genocide also had an undeniable impact on the mental health of many Rwandans. Genocide survivors often had post-traumatic stress disorder (PTSD) because of the things they had witnessed and experienced. Killers also suffered the mental effects of having taken part in the genocide. According to witness accounts, some killers would shout for help for no apparent reason, as if tormented by the infants they had killed. Some refused to seek medical treatment. Having lost their humanity, or more likely, the Holy Spirit of God, they could not trust the international community missions to help them as refugees. They thought they would try to kill them. I imagine such an existence would be a worse punishment than the one Cain received after he had killed his brother Abel.

After some three to four weeks, the authorities told everybody to go back to their respective homes. Those who still had homes to return to went back right away. Those whose homes had been destroyed remained in the camp for some time. There was so much confusion. There were many children without parents, men without wives, and women without husbands. Many people had lost everything they owned.

There was still a lot of suffering, and no help could be counted on apart from turning to the God of heaven. Though some had rejected Him, and others had never really known Him, in this situation, some people learned to depend on God alone. After learning lessons the hard way, many have continued to rely on Him even to this day.

17

Learning Lessons the Hard Way

All these people were still living by faith when they died. They did not receive the things promised; they only saw them and welcomed them from a distance, admitting that they were foreigners and strangers on earth. People who say such things show that they are looking for a country of their own. . . . Therefore God is not ashamed to be called their God, for he has prepared a city for them.
—Hebrews 11:13, 14, 16

What happened in Rwanda in 1994 was, and still is, a puzzle to Rwandans and the international community. It is strange when one hears about more than one million people being killed within only three months. That is a death rate of over ten thousand persons per day in a small country.

People have done research and written papers about the Rwandan genocide, yet how such a thing could happen still remains a mystery. Rwanda is a country where there was social integration among the people and intermarriages between Hutus and Tutsis were common. In addition, almost everyone was Christian. That fact alone raises more questions than answers.

It is even more difficult to determine why God would allow this to happen. Was He still in control of the situation in Rwanda? Or did He totally abandon the people there? Had He left them in the hands of the devil, who was doing whatever he wanted at this time? These types of questions need to be addressed.

It took time for me to accept what had happened. It was so difficult to understand then, and I do not claim to understand fully now. During the genocide, my own eyes saw the basest evil. Killers had taken the lives of so many people. But I would not allow myself to think of the possibility that what happened where I was had happened in every other place in the country.

As I came out of the bush, I thought there might have been places in the country where the people had resisted the genocidal ideology and the propaganda of the government and militia. I hoped my home village might be such an exception. Because of the social ties that existed in the area, I couldn't imagine that my neighbors could have killed my family.

The victims of the genocide probably never thought that such a terrible thing could happen until it did. Had they sensed the danger, they would have left the country before it was too late.

A small country, measuring 26,338 square kilometers (10,169 square miles), Rwanda is laid out in such a way that people could have run away to neighboring countries to save their lives. Had the Tutsis known the danger they were in, they could have walked for several hours and made it to safety across the border.

As I reflected on this, I came to some kind of understanding concerning why people didn't leave before it was too late to do so. In many parts of the country, there was a high level of trust among most people. People believed in the goodness of those around them, because they were Christians and were related through various family ties. Because of this misplaced trust, it took victims by surprise to discover that their neighbors could turn into killers after a simple political mobilization.

Although almost everyone in Rwanda was a Christian, something essential was missing. So-called Christians may have believed Bible truths, but they lacked true conversion.

Victims thought a church building would be a safe refuge. But gathering in these supposed sanctuaries simply made it easier for the militia, who regarded nothing as sacred, to find them together. It was in churches that the militia slaughtered hundreds of thousands of people. Sometimes, bulldozers destroyed the church buildings as militiamen tried to bury both the living and those already dead inside. Church members, along with many pastors and priests, took part in the killing.

I can't completely comprehend why a God of love would allow this to happen in Rwanda. It is almost impossible to prove the love of God to the victims of the genocide. However, it is my belief that we can somewhat understand what took place in the light of the cosmic war that is going on between good and evil (see Revelation 12:7). In this war, God seeks to save as many people as possible for His kingdom. As He does so, different battles are going on, during which God saves His chosen ones, even when the plan of the devil is to destroy them. Based on biblical truth, physical death is not always a loss to God in this war. It is sometimes a gain, regardless of the death one dies.

Talking about John the Baptist, Jesus testified that of all those born of women, there was no one greater than him (see Luke 7:28). Yet Herod beheaded John (see Matthew 14:1–12). This could suggest that John's death had nothing to do with God not loving him. If this was the case, the suffering of those who die by acts of atrocity is not because God does not love them or because He has abandoned them.

Based on all the testimonies I have heard, many who died during the genocide in Rwanda had the opportunity to settle their spiritual matters with God before they were killed. Though most of them died in horrible ways, they had time to prepare for their last minutes of life. When I think about these, I believe that for some, their final minutes must have been more precious to them than any they had experienced during their whole lives. Though they were abandoned by the world and hunted down by killers, God had not forsaken them.

Many stories refer to the fact that individuals were praying and reading the Word of God in the days before their deaths as they gathered in church buildings and on the tops of mountains. Some were lonely and abandoned in ceilings of houses or in bushes, waiting for their killers. Having no other refuge than God, they put their lives into His hands and asked for forgiveness. Knowing the forgiving nature of God, I believe that just as He forgave the thief on the cross, He understood these persons in their tribulations and accepted their petitions.

When I am about to lament and complain, one thing that often causes me to rejoice is the case of my sister, the firstborn in our family. After she sought refuge in the Roman Catholic Church in Kibuye, a time came when the people hiding there were all asked to pray, each one according to his or her own religious beliefs, because there was no more safety and death was coming soon.

An eyewitness told me that my sister, having heard this, rushed back to see her husband who had remained in their home about a kilometer away. According to the account, they heard her saying that she had to see her husband so she could ask him to repent and recommit himself into God's hands before they died.

I have heard stories of men, women, youths, and even children who took time enough to pray, repenting of their sins, forgiving their killers, and even praying for them before they were killed. All these people died with clear consciences, forgiven of all their sins, which might not have been the case had they continued to live on this earth.

It is possible to see that the way the genocide ended showed that God was in control. It did not end the way the killers had planned. They had thought to eliminate all their victims and continue to rule the country. While they were singing, *"Tubatsembatsembe"* ("Let us finish them all"), God put a limit on their time and evil deeds. At the end of that time, there was a remnant of survivors whom God had saved in miraculous ways.

Had the militia succeeded in all their plans, the country today would be under the rule of killers and no one thereafter would have been able to call sin by its name. Among killers, there would be the belief that evil can triumph, and among all Rwandans there would be confusion. Having their evil plans thwarted left the militiamen running for their lives. Maybe some came back on their senses and repented, realizing that they had tried to fight a mightier God.

How I wish the genocide of Rwanda could be a lesson for everyone else in the world! We need to understand the real nature of nominal Christianity. Before the genocide, I preached in many places. I witnessed thousands and thousands giving their lives to Jesus. I saw them attending church and singing as if they were real believers in the true God.

Before the 1994 genocide, Christians in Rwanda were just as good as most of those we see around us today. Within a few weeks, however, I saw many of these become involved in atrocities that no human mind could comprehend. This helped me learn that "we wrestle not against flesh and blood, but against principalities, against powers, against the rulers of the darkness of this world, against spiritual wickedness in high places" (Ephesians 6:12, KJV). We need to understand that real conversion is a change of heart and not mere adherence to a set of doctrines.

Everyone who believes in the Word of God knows that we are living in evil days. We must be certain we have deep roots of faith in Christ. Without a firm conviction, based on a real relationship of true love and genuine commitment to God, there is no assurance that one will remain on the side of God when the time of trouble comes.

Jesus warned, "Be careful, or your hearts will be weighed down with carousing, drunkenness and the anxieties of life, and that day will close on you suddenly like a trap. For it will come on all those who live on the face of the whole earth. Be always on the watch, and pray that you may be able to escape all that is about to happen, and that you may be able to stand before the Son of Man" (Luke 21:34–36).

18

Conquering the Enemy's Territory

One night the Lord spoke to Paul in a vision:
"Do not be afraid; keep on speaking, do not be silent.
For I am with you, and no one is going to attack
and harm you, because I have many people in this city."
—Acts 18:9, 10

Once we had stopped our moving around the country, the most important thing for me was to find my family members. I was in Ntongwe, one hundred kilometers (sixty-two miles) from my home village. I had many family members, and I had heard that they had scattered. Where was I to begin? I decided to go back to Kigali and then go home to Kibuye. I wanted to find out if my relatives had survived.

Getting to Kigali was difficult. I had no money, and transportation was scarce. There were only a few military trucks and cars. My friend, Jules, agreed to accompany me on foot to Ruhango and later to Kigali.

Memories of the brutal killings in Kigali haunted me. Who had been killed and who had escaped? Was there a church or were any church members left? These questions crossed my mind as I traveled back to Kigali.

After my arrival in Kigali, the first person I met was one of my former colleagues, an elder in the church I used to attend before the genocide. I was glad he had survived. He updated me on some of our church members. It pleased me to know they were still alive.

Kigali was no longer the same. The militia had destroyed houses and damaged roads. There were bullet holes everywhere. One difference I appreciated was that there were no more killers in the streets! The roadblocks I had crossed while trying to run to Gitarama were no more.

I felt like one who had risen from the dead. Things had also changed for me. The only shoes I had were the old ones I'd found in the bush. I was wearing the same clothing I had worn since fleeing my home months before. I looked as tired as I felt.

Ever since the time I had been in the bush, I had almost lost my voice. While hiding there, we could not talk with a full, normal voice for about three months, and after we came out, the condition continued. Jules tried to encourage me to speak at a normal volume, but it was in vain. To myself, I thought I was speaking well, but I was whispering whenever I tried to speak. I was so used to not speaking above a whisper for such a long time that it was hard for me to know when I was doing it.

The house I used to stay in was now desolate. Killers and opportunists had forced open all the houses and taken everything away. There were signs that people had been staying in the home after our flight. Though there was nothing in our house, church members in Kigali were generous to us. Soon after we arrived, they provided for our needs. Some brought food to our home, and someone took me to the market for clothing and shoes. I got a new suit and a tie, which I intended to wear when preaching.

Until this time, my priority had been survival. I was not even sure what was going on elsewhere. But now that I was free, my thoughts turned toward my home village. I became worried about what was going on there. While the genocide had stopped in our area, the RPF had not yet rescued Kibuye and all the western part of the country.

While I was eagerly planning to see my family, I met an elder from Kibuye who had come to Kigali. "Nobody in your family survived," he told me. My heart sank in terrible sorrow.

"They have all been killed," he repeated. My father, six of my siblings, nieces, nephews, cousins, aunts, and uncles were no more. Only my sister in the Congo was still alive. Every relative I had in Rwanda was now dead.

This man explained how he had tried to hide my sister, Athaly, in vain. My heart ached to learn how she'd suffered. In our village, people knew her well because of her kindness. Many neighbors had given her friendly nicknames in recognition of her generosity. She gave food and clothes to the poor. This man had tried to hide her in his house when many people were being killed. When the militia found out she was in his house, they came to kill her.

Conquering the Enemy's Territory

My sister overheard the killers threatening the man who had hidden her. Realizing he was in danger of being killed because he would not cooperate with them, she came out from her hiding place under the bed to face them. She stood before them without fear and said, "Let anyone who has something against me step up and kill me." No one had the nerve to take her life.

The militiamen were among those whose families she had been assisting and providing for. At her words, they all withdrew, but soon they returned. They had convinced one of their gang to kill my sister by promising him incentives. After stripping her of her clothes, he cut her into pieces without pity.

There were no tears in my eyes as I listened to the elder tell me what had happened. I stared ahead in dumb silence. For a while, I wondered why God would spare my life but not the lives of my relatives. Why had God allowed this to happen? Why had He not let me die too? There seemed to be no meaning in me being alive. I no longer had my nephews, who were the same age as I. Words can never express what I felt upon hearing the most discouraging stories of my life! I felt all alone.

For a while, my heart pounded against my chest, I found it hard to breathe, and I pressed my lips together whenever I thought of my family. I tried to picture my relatives, one after the other, in my thoughts. My mind wandered back to when I last saw them. I remembered visiting them about four months prior to this time. I also thought about all I had been through since then and wondered how I was still alive.

Then, something struck my mind, and I realized I was alive because of many miracles! I understood that I should not have survived all that had happened in our country. Putting the pieces together, I saw that I did not belong to myself and that my survival had nothing to do with my family. I was a miracle, and God had spared my life for a purpose. This realization strengthened my heart again, and I prayed, thanking God and asking Him to help me understand what His purpose for my life was.

I also came to realize that, while I loved my family so much, God loved them much more. As a young man, I missed them terribly, and even today I still miss them so much. I wish I had spent more time sharing with them, as do all Rwandans who lost their loved ones. This was not possible as our time together was cut short.

None of us knew that soon we would never see each other again. But I believe it won't be long before we meet again when Jesus comes. Then, there will be no more Hutus or Tutsis. My family members completed their life journeys and now wait for the call of the Life-Giver, when the dead will come out of their graves never to die again.

I decided not to go home. I found some comfort in listening to many others who had experienced similar losses. Meanwhile, I continued my church leadership position in the Remera SDA Church in Kigali, where I had been serving before the genocide started. I shared my testimony and preached almost every week in my church. I also received several invitations to preach around the country.

In my preaching engagements, I would testify about how God had performed miracle after miracle to save me throughout the time of the genocide. I also conducted several evangelistic campaigns. In serving God, I lost sight of my own problems and any desire for comfort and focused on giving glory to Him. During this time, I could not think of my village. I was trying to forget about home, though from time to time, there were things that reminded me of my family. My main concern was God's work. Turning my attention there interrupted my painful thoughts.

While some of us were busy preaching, others were preoccupied with trying to gain material possessions. Looting was still going on, with thieves breaking into abandoned houses to enrich themselves. Dealing in stolen items during and after the genocide was common.

Meanwhile, many survivors were still trying to recover from the effects of what they had suffered. Some had survived with serious injuries. Some were still in hospitals, maimed, with cuts on their heads or more often on their necks. But the majority, wounded in their hearts and minds, were only just beginning to suffer the painful internal consequences of all they had witnessed and experienced.

Those of us who were preaching shared the miracles God had done and tried to encourage those with wounded hearts. The demands were so many that answering all of them was difficult for me. I had not yet made a full recovery from the aftermath of the genocide myself, and I felt I should pause and rest for a while. I also wanted to make a living to supply my own needs.

But there was no time to rest. I often had to preach, contrary to my desire, because it was an urgent time. I remember one day; we had concluded an evangelistic campaign in Kicukiro, where we intended to plant a new church.

Conquering the Enemy's Territory

We held an elders' council and made plans to have an evangelistic campaign in a different city where our help was needed.

Since I was still tired, we appointed as speaker a man well-known for his bravery in trying to save some Tutsis who were being hunted. He had hidden more than a hundred, including the man who was then the president of the Seventh-day Adventist Church in Rwanda. After we appointed this man to the task, he said he would not like to go to preach without me.

I tried to argue that I shouldn't go since I lacked energy and needed to recover, but he would not agree. The day for the evangelistic effort to begin came before I had made my final decision. I was still trying to recuperate and had planned to join him later. When I woke up that Friday morning before the program was to start, I felt even sicker.

My fever was high, and my body was shaking. Then I remembered that I had committed myself to serve God in all circumstances. I reasoned that maybe my weakness was because of my resistance to serve with my whole heart. After praying, I made my way to the site of the meetings that day. It was difficult, because I could not even sit up in the car. I lay down in the back seat throughout the journey. God performed a miracle, for as soon as we arrived at the meeting site, the fever left me! We preached the gospel and baptized about 230 people within only one week! We had planned to preach for two weeks, but the local authorities prevented us from doing so because of security reasons.

As I kept hearing news from my home village, I decided I would go and at least see the mountains, which I was missing so much. I did not go to the village itself though. I stayed in a nearby village with the president of the Seventh-day Adventist Church in the area. Word had spread that when the villagers saw a survivor coming toward them, they might still attempt to kill him, because they thought he was coming for revenge or to claim compensation for what thieves had stolen during the genocide. Because it was not safe, I stayed about fifteen kilometers (nine miles) away and delayed going home.

The morning after my arrival, I met the only survivor from a family related to my brother-in-law. She alone had survived while some of my family members were being slaughtered before her eyes. A soldier who had been her brother's friend protected this girl. He had come to this her home to rescue his friend.

When he saw her being taken to the place where they intended to kill her and others, he recognized her and stepped in to protect her in place of her brother, who had already been killed by the militia. Turning his gun against the militiamen, he told them that if they were not willing to release this Tutsi girl, he was ready to die himself after killing all of them!

The militiamen found the risk to their own lives too great to go against this determined soldier, and they released the girl, but they still killed the rest of their captives. As they were leaving, the soldier explained to her that the reason he was ready to die with her in order to try to save her life was because of what her brother had done for him as a friend.

After much suffering while trying to protect her, the soldier sent her at last into Congo, through Lake Kivu. This girl had witnessed the killing of some of my family members, and she gave me details of how they died. She described how some of them died in the Roman Catholic Church in Kibuye.

The girl also told me how one of my nephews, injured when the militia threw grenades into the church, had escaped, along with some other nephews and nieces. His bleeding from a severe wound on his neck was profuse. The others begged him not to follow them. They knew he was already dying and that if he followed them, he would leave a trail of blood that would lead the killers to wherever they were hiding. But he was hoping to survive and could not just sit and wait for death. What they feared became a reality. The militia followed the blood until they found and finished them all.

She showed me the hill on which the militia had mounted machine guns to make sure that nobody made it out of the church alive. As I listened to the details of my family's deaths, it saddened me beyond words. After about two days, I decided that returning to Kigali would bring a sense of calm back to my life.

19

Loving the Killers of My Family

*Then I saw "a new heaven and a new earth," for the first heaven
and the first earth had passed away, and there was no longer any sea.
I saw the Holy City, the new Jerusalem, coming down out of heaven from
God, prepared as a bride beautifully dressed for her husband. And I heard
a loud voice from the throne saying, "Look! God's dwelling place is now
among the people, and he will dwell with them. They will be his people,
and God himself will be with them and be their God. 'He will wipe every
tear from their eyes. There will be no more death' or mourning or crying
or pain, for the old order of things has passed away."
He who was seated on the throne said, "I am making everything
new!" Then he said, "Write this down, for these words
are trustworthy and true."
He said to me: "It is done. I am the Alpha and the Omega,
the Beginning and the End."*

—Revelation 21:1–6

While I stayed in the church president's house in Kibuye, he requested that
I come and help him serve the church as the Youth and Education director.
He reasoned that since this was my home province, I would be helpful in the
ministry. This was not an easy request. I didn't want to stay in this place due
to the painful memories of my family.

I felt like a stranger where I used to feel at home. Before the genocide, I
would meet my relatives everywhere, but now they were all gone. Even those
who knew me would avoid me out of hatred or fear. I left Kibuye without
giving him my final answer.

Preaching From the Grave

While in Kigali, I reflected on how God had rescued me from critical situations. He had saved me for a purpose! With this conviction, I was ready to consider the request the president of our church in Kibuye had made earlier. I accepted the appointment to be the Youth and Education director of our mission.

My responsibilities would include visiting over 240 churches in the whole mission district. With a determination to serve God with all my heart, I embarked on my assignment, trusting God for guidance. I followed a tight itinerary that took me away from Kigali for two months at a time. I enjoyed my work, and it thrilled me to see people accepting Jesus. But I still had not dared to go to my home village. My courage was lacking!

I continued serving God in other villages where people knew nothing about me until after I identified myself. For a while, I felt I was OK, trying to dodge my "enemies"! But something was tormenting me. There was a voice I did not want to listen to. Before the genocide, I had prayed for a job and promised to God that once I got one, I would use my salary to buy literature and go back to my home village to preach the gospel to the people there. But it is interesting that even when we say we love God and want to serve Him, there is often some selfishness or self-interest tainting our motives.

When I first made that vow, I was thinking of my village and had considered it mine only because of my relatives living there. After the militia killed them all, I did not consider myself indebted to God regarding the vow I had made. Besides, there were real enemies there who might kill me if they saw me. Apart from the unsafe situation, I reasoned that no one would be willing to listen to what I had to say. Some had killed, and some were the relatives of killers. I could not know who was innocent, and they could not know if I knew of their innocence. I felt they were all in the same basket. All were enemies and killers of Tutsis and my family.

I tried to console myself with the fact that I was already doing something for God, but an inner voice kept telling me, "You must go!" I had no peace with my conscience. In my heart, I knew I needed to fulfill the vow I'd made years ago.

Tensions were high. I had heard stories of some survivors who had gone back to my home village and their narrow escapes when hostile Hutus tried to kill them. The consciences of many were still dealing with dark memories. In this area, they had not buried all the dead. Across the hills and valleys lay

144

Loving the Killers of My Family

the skulls of many Tutsis. I faced a difficult challenge.

One day, I prayed and made plans in alignment with my conscience. I was at last willing to preach to the people who had killed my father, brother, five sisters, other relatives, and most of the Tutsis in that area. As soon as I reached this decision, I informed my church president. He could not believe it! He knew the struggle I had been going through. I also informed the pastor of the church in my home village of my plans to visit and asked him to announce to the church members that I would be coming. I wanted to prepare them ahead of time for my arrival so it would not shock them when they saw me.

There was a lot of shame among the church members, as I found out later when I talked with them. Some had killed; some had children or husbands who had taken part in hunting down Tutsis. Others had confiscated our fields or looted our properties. There were also many who had done nothing to hide their Tutsi neighbors.

As I shared my plan with my friends and some church members, many of them met me with stiff resistance. Most of my friends found it absurd that I wanted to take the news of salvation to people who had killed my own relatives. Where was the fairness? Wasn't God expecting too much from a mortal? I remember one young lady, a genocide survivor, questioning whether these kinds of people could repent and receive forgiveness. When I said I thought so, she said she would like to kill them also if God could forgive her of the same sin!

By this time, however, no one would ever dissuade me from going. I felt determined, and I believed the people of my village were God's children who needed His mercy and forgiveness. They needed the salvation only God can provide. I would preach and leave the results to Him. I devoted time to prayer, entreating God for the Holy Spirit to do His part as I would do mine. The pastor assigned to my village arranged everything I needed for the evangelistic meetings I intended to hold.

As the day drew closer, I packed my clothes, books, sermons, and a megaphone. I arrived at my village on Friday evening and stayed with one of our church members, who was a medical doctor working at the nearby clinic. Early Saturday morning, with my Bible in hand, I headed to the church. Congregants were already in Sabbath School.

I looked around; where I used to see hundreds of Tutsis, many of whom were my family members, I saw none of them! I sensed the unhappiness and

Preaching From the Grave

resentment that was now present. All the people who did not know me were looking at me as if I were a stranger in my home church.

I felt I did not have to be insensitive to my dilemma or be an angel to preach to God's people and do the work I knew God was calling me to do. I had forgiven them and had no resentment toward anyone. There is no wrong I would ever have done to harm any of them, but so far, they were not my friends. They were still my enemies, but I had a message from God to deliver to them.

The meetings started that Saturday afternoon. I had given instructions to the pastor regarding where I wanted to hold the meetings. I didn't want them held in the church. We were to convene on a hill in the open air. That afternoon, I saw mostly women and children but few men. They were afraid and thought I was after revenge or felt too ashamed to come to the meetings. It was the same among the visitors who were not Seventh-day Adventists; only women and children would come.

As I preached, I presented God's love for sinners, among whom I also considered myself. I assured them that my love for God and for them was the sole reason I could come to them, explaining that it would have been impossible to have come there otherwise.

I told them, "I wish my relatives were alive to hear me speak the Word of God, but since they are all gone, I still had to come and fulfill my vow to God. The Lord has a plan for your lives, and that is why He has given you the chance to live. My prayer is that you will not hear the young man you knew before, but see in me a messenger of the Almighty God."

After my first sermon that afternoon, the news of my presence spread throughout the village and the surrounding communities. "A genocide survivor is preaching!" God worked miracles. Every day brought more people to listen to the Word of God, and everyone who came invited several others, including members of their families. Men started coming with their spouses. Soon, there was excitement among us all as we sensed that we were no longer enemies. "Amen" reverberated throughout the valley of Gisiza, where I was preaching, as we praised God, who alone could accomplish such a miracle.

Night after night, for eight nights, many people streamed in to hear me preach. At the end of the evangelistic effort, I invited those in attendance to give themselves to Jesus. About 120 people accepted Jesus as their personal Savior and were baptized.

Loving the Killers of My Family

Among the converts was the man who had killed one of my sisters. I gave him a Bible for a present. I praised God that He had empowered me to do the unimaginable. What was happening was nothing for which I could take credit. Had it been up to my natural inclination, I would not have gone! But the God who had protected my life had a higher purpose for me, and I was glad He had spoken through me to His children, despite my weaknesses. My heart was at peace, because I had fulfilled my vow at last.

After this experience, I felt I should do something more. People had wounded hearts, and there was a need for spiritual healing. I thought I could help to facilitate reconciliation between the few Tutsis who had survived and the guilt-ridden Hutus. After preaching in my village, I expanded my evangelistic efforts. People were very receptive to the preaching of the gospel, and I wanted to take advantage of this opportunity to reach out to as many people as I could.

I decided to hold another evangelistic meeting in the Rubengera open-air market, about ten kilometers (six miles) from my village. My strategy was to use several large speakers to ensure that as many people as possible could hear me preach. My main targets were the twenty or more churches close to the market.

After consulting with the pastor responsible for the work of evangelism in the area, he and I decided to go to the local government leaders to apply for authorization. The church elders also pledged their support for the work. We reasoned that if we gained approval for our plans, there would be no need to invite people to come. The market was a place where thousands of people went at least twice a week to shop. We wanted to start the evangelistic effort on one of the market days so that as people noticed our meeting while they visited the market, they would share with others what was taking place.

We invited choirs from the surrounding churches, and even from Kigali, to sing. I also enlisted the support of the youth to assist with the follow-up work. We expected unity to emerge as people worked side by side and invited their neighbors to the meetings.

Having put everything in order, a church elder and I went to see the bourmestre (mayor) of the city. I arrived before the elder and entered the mayor's office. We had already prayed and believed God was with us.

As soon as I introduced the idea to the mayor, it was like he already had an answer prepared to give me. There was no resistance at all to our having the meetings, but he wanted to offer me a soccer stadium which was far away from people's homes. I had thought about that option before and had decided never to conduct an evangelistic effort there if I wanted it to succeed. I told him I needed the market.

"The market is a public place for shopping and not for preaching," he clarified.

"Sir, I know this, but following what has happened in Rwanda, my plan is to reach out to as many people as possible. If I go to the stadium, only a few people will come," I persisted.

"There are all kinds of people in the market, not just your church members," he said.

Speaking with confidence, I explained, "My spiritual healing program is not just for Adventists but for every Rwandan. That is why I would like to use the market. This is to help people, and you will see the final results!"

After thinking about it for a moment, he almost agreed, but he still had a question about feasibility. I told him that I had spotted one part of the market which was being used for selling animals such as goats and sheep. It was a beautiful area with short grass. The setup would be convenient for public speaking as everyone in attendance could see with no obstruction. Our meetings would start in the afternoon. All the animals were usually sold by noon, so the area would be available for our intended purpose when we needed it.

Having heard me for a while, it still seemed like he wanted to deny me the authorization without giving a direct answer. Attempting to discourage me, he said the charge was thirty thousand Rwandan francs for the use of the space. This was an exorbitant amount to pay. I tried to negotiate, knowing I was at risk of being denied my request altogether. He finally accepted ten thousand francs, which I also did not have, because I did not expect him to charge any fees.

"If you can't pay this amount, please get out of my office," he said with a degree of impatience. "I can't help you anymore!"

This was a crucial moment. I told him I would bring the money. To be honest, I did not know where to get it! There were no cell phones and no way of communicating to anyone my immediate need for this money. But I believed God was in control. I walked out the door without knowing where to go. As soon as I left his office, I met the church elder who had delayed to come with me into the building and had stayed outside.

Loving the Killers of My Family

"What is going on?" the elder asked.

"I need money! Please give me money!" I exclaimed.

"How much?" he inquired.

"Ten thousand francs," I told him quickly.

Just then, with no other question, the elder pulled out of his pocket the ten thousand francs that I needed. This was a large amount of money in Rwanda in those days, especially in a place like Rubengera. It was another answer from God.

We were all excited and ready to start our meetings in this most strategic area. With little effort, we would reach thousands of people who had never attended church or would never have responded to our invitations!

On Saturday afternoon, instead of going home, our church members from the surrounding churches in the area converged on the market. Everyone had their Bibles in hand. It was unusual for traders to see about a thousand people moving through the market, all going in the same direction, doing no shopping.

We had spotted several electric poles from which we could hang speakers so they would project our voices as far as possible. As choirs started to sing in the market, those who were selling stopped and joined us. They did so because all their customers were in our audience. Before I preached, I prayed that the Lord would empower me with His Spirit so I could speak without fear. The Lord answered my prayer. Instead of the numbers decreasing, our attendance increased daily, even when there were no market activities.

I preached for an entire week with no problems. People were giving their lives to Jesus, and I was thankful to the Lord. One day, however, as I was finishing the evangelistic meetings, people from a different church organization came and told us that since we were in a public market, they should also have the right to address the people.

A group of Muslims also came, saying they had their own people there and wanted to address them too. I requested several elders to deal with the problem. I knew Satan was not happy to see people surrendering their lives to Jesus.

Another interruption happened when a man asked for a microphone to give his testimony after I'd made an altar call. The things he said at first were positive. He told about how the messages being preached had touched him. Then, all at once, he deviated.

Preaching From the Grave

"I am wondering why people are not coming to the front the way I did," he said. "People need to repent. I can identify many of you here who were involved in the killings during the genocide. I am looking at some of you right now. Surrender yourselves to Jesus!"

As soon as I realized that his speech could prevent people from coming to the meetings, I promptly, yet carefully, stopped him. I wanted people to continue coming. I wanted them to hear the Word of God so they could repent without intimidation.

Listening to that man's short testimony, it was obvious he had been through a lot. He had seen people killed during the genocide and sounded quite traumatized. Though he seemed sincere in his intention, our purpose was to help people go through the healing process. We wanted to allow people to go through the process of repentance on their own, without coercion.

The Lord blessed our program. We were so excited as we baptized about 220 people, with several hundred others getting ready for baptism soon. God had been with me. People were no longer my enemies. They rejoiced to see me, and I felt happy to minister to and work with them as we united to fulfill the Lord's commission.

20

An American Refuses to Leave

"If my people, who are called by my name, will humble themselves and pray and seek my face and turn from their wicked ways, then I will hear from heaven, and I will forgive their sin and will heal their land."
—2 Chronicles 7:14

Preceding the genocide, many expatriates had come to serve the Rwandan people during the time of the mounting crisis. Among them was the United Nations Assistance Mission for Rwanda (UNAMIR), a group of about one thousand seven hundred heavily armed soldiers. There were also civil rights activists and missionaries from different countries.

When the genocide started, all these people were in danger since heavy fighting was going on. Everyone had to choose between continuing to serve the poor Rwandans, who were now in their most serious need, or vacating the country. This was a difficult time. The vast majority of foreigners in Rwanda headed for the airport and flew out of the country for their own security.

What has been difficult for Rwandans and the international community at large to understand was the behavior of the UNAMIR. Right after the death of the president, about three thousand people living near their military base ran into their camp. They thought that under the UN's protection, they would find safety from the militia's attack. For some time, they felt secure there, while militiamen were gathering around the outskirts of the UNAMIR military camp, waiting and watching like hungry lions stalking their prey. But in a few days, the UN army packed up to leave! It was a shock to the Tutsis who had sought shelter there. The killers still surrounded the camp, while thousands of other people were being killed in the vicinity.

Knowing that death was inevitable, the Rwandans who had sought refuge decided not to just let it happen. Many lay down on the roads to hinder the heavy UNAMIR armed vehicles trying to pass. But this was useless. The UN army fired into the air and cleared the roads within a few minutes.

After their departure, desperate Tutsis tried to run toward the zone controlled by the RPF (Rwandan Patriotic Front), but soon the armed militia and government soldiers turned them back. They led the Tutsis to a place called Nyanza and slaughtered them there all that afternoon. It was almost too late when the RPA (Rwandan Patriotic Army) reached Nyanza. Of the three thousand or so Tutsis, only about two hundred survived to tell the story. Since I was living in Kicukiro, my friends and I had also thought we should try to seek protection from the UNAMIR. I thank God that He did not allow me to go there.

In the surrounding villages near the UN military camp in Kicukiro, the militia killed about eight thousand other Tutsis. Some eleven thousand people are buried at the genocide memorial at Nyanza (Kicukiro). For Rwandans, the eleven thousand buried in Kicukiro, the fourteen thousand buried about three kilometers (two miles) from that site, and the more than 250,000 buried in the Gisozi Genocide Memorial are a constant reminder of the UN's failure to protect. Not only had the UN forces failed but so did the international community of believers in God, who did not intervene when fellow human beings were being killed.

In contrast with most of the UN forces and the many missionaries who left Rwanda, Carl Wilkens, who was the director of the Adventist Disaster Relief Agency (ADRA) in 1994, stood firm. He was the only American who stayed during the genocide in Rwanda. He was ready to sacrifice his life for the people he had come to serve, rather than abandon them at the time when they needed him most.

When the US embassy said all Americans should leave, there were already two people who had sought refuge in his house. Carl knew that leaving them behind would mean their death. He prayed about the matter together with his wife and children. They agreed his family would move to Nairobi, while he remained behind so he could protect the ones in desperate need.

Going out each day into the blood-filled streets of Kigali, Carl faced the militiamen who were killing innocent men, women, and children. He helped

An American Refuses to Leave

save the lives of many people in Rwanda. He had obtained a document from the mayor of the city that allowed him to aid the orphanage in Kigali, as there were many there who were dying of hunger and thirst.

After our country's tragedy, the president of the world Seventh-day Adventist Church visited Rwanda. The president of the country could not come to our meeting because of another commitment, so he sent a high-ranking government official to represent him. We assembled in a hotel in Kigali. The government representative told the president of the Adventist Church and those present, "If all Christians in Rwanda had been like Carl, what happened in Rwanda might not have happened."

He continued, "I saw Carl, a white man, during the most dangerous moments of the conflict in our country. He was running between the two armies during heavy fighting, trying to save the wounded, searching for those in hiding, and bringing them to safety. This man could have been killed, because he was definitely in a danger zone, but God showed him that He is always with those that selflessly serve Him." The representative's words expressed the sentiments of many Rwandans, especially those who are alive because of Carl's efforts.

A woman told me how Carl had helped her during the genocide. A Hutu pastor had hidden this woman and her daughter for weeks. When the pastor heard that the Rwandan Patriotic Front army was fast approaching, he ran away, leaving them behind to fend for themselves.

Before leaving, the pastor prayed for them and entrusted them into the hands of God. Soon after the pastor left, Carl came and took the mother and her child to safety. He saved them, along with several other Tutsis who had been hiding in a baptistry in the Nyamirambo SDA Church. His intervention also helped to save hundreds of orphan children by providing them sustenance and helping to keep the militia from killing them.

For the last few years, Carl has been sharing his story around the globe to inspire and equip people to "enter the world of the other." His purpose is to help as many young men and women as possible to understand that one person can make a difference and that individuals sow seeds of change when they look outside of themselves, reach out to one another, and live for each other.*

Before 1994, I did not know Carl well. We became familiar to each other

* See details available on Carl's personal website: http://www.worldoutsidemyshoes.org.

after the genocide, as I was preaching reconciliation and love for God and our fellow humans. While still in Kibuye, I often invited him to come assist me and, though a high-ranking leader in the church, he would never think of sending someone else. I remember him bringing his family over, climbing the mountains, riding a motorcycle, preaching to thousands of young people, and donating roofing sheets to hundreds of churches destroyed by the war.

One of the most important contributions to my mission happened when I left Kibuye and went back to Kigali to continue my studies. While in Kibuye, I thought of spreading the preaching efforts I had made in my home village to over two hundred churches. My purpose was to empower young people, who would extend my efforts to their churches. But I abandoned this idea when I got the chance to further my studies in theology in Kigali.

Almost a year and a half had passed since I had started the work in Kibuye, and I was now moving to Kigali, which was a different mission field. I worried about the work I was leaving behind. But as I attended the church in Kigali, I soon realized that the need was even more urgent in this war-torn city. Before the genocide, there were many laypeople involved in evangelism. But after the genocide, most church members became distracted by the cares of life.

Many Hutus and Tutsis who used to be active in the church were now dormant. In the past, they had organized evangelistic efforts and had managed, as lay members, to baptize thousands of people. They had done a great work in Rwanda. The difference that Rwanda had made in terms of church growth was largely a result of their efforts.

After the genocide, some felt seriously wounded by their fellow Christians while others felt shame or fear following the atrocities that had taken place. The love of many had waxed cold (see Matthew 24:12). Everyone was wondering what would happen next. The church was united in appearance, but in reality, it was divided and cold. Some had even resolved not to attend church, reasoning that it was in the churches that people were killed, sometimes by fellow believers. I felt there was a need to do something about this.

Carl played a role I will never forget. I was just a busy college student, trying to work on my Hebrew and Greek assignments. Being enrolled in school full-time, I had no money to do what I wished to do. But God had prepared Carl for this work. I did not plan for him to help, but he intervened right when I was desperate and took over a big part of the responsibility.

An American Refuses to Leave

My plan was to use the youth to help conduct over forty evangelistic efforts in Kigali. But since I was just a freshman in college with no responsibility in the church organization, I went to the president of the church in Kigali and introduced him to the plan. He agreed that it was a good idea, though he skeptically questioned how it could ever be possible.

We were planning to concentrate our efforts on one section of the city before moving to another. The program would last one week. We mobilized all twenty churches in Kigali to get involved and assigned at least two churches to each site to reach out to the people. Two or more choirs were to sing at each site every day. I had asked one of my professors to come and train the lay preachers who would carry out the work.

I felt highly impressed with the work we would accomplish, but because of my lack of experience, I did not know there would be a need for some financial means to carry out the work. The problem came to my attention when I sent copies of the program to different churches around Kigali. Many questions came back regarding the legitimacy of the cause I proposed. "What do you represent?" some people asked. "Who are you to think you'll be able to do these things?" others wanted to know. But the most important questions were those that dealt with feasibility. I realized that my preparation was lacking.

There was a need for tents to hold thousands of people, and not only in one place but sometimes in over ten sites at the same time. There was a need for sound systems to address the people. We also needed money to transport choir members, buy literature to distribute to the visitors, print invitation cards and posters, and pay for other needs that would arise. Despite all these issues, I believed God had the answers.

I prayed and went to visit Carl at his office in the ADRA building. He could spend only a few minutes with me because he had many appointments. I quickly told him about the plans for the evangelistic campaigns and our need for tents and sound systems. It seemed like he could not understand me well. My English was not good enough to give a detailed explanation within such a short time. His kindness amazed me when he offered to come to my dormitory at school that evening to carefully listen to me.

That evening, the ADRA director was at the college looking for me. There was no living room, just dormitory rooms. I wondered how I could take him to my room, but since no other options were available, we went there and sat on my small bed.

Preaching From the Grave

After I shared the detailed plans, Carl promised to provide the sound systems and tents for the meetings! But this was nothing compared to what he was going to do! God had brought him to me for a purpose. I hesitated before telling him the biggest obstacle we faced.

"Sir," I said solemnly, "what I am trying to do may not work, and I may not even need your donations."

"Why?" he asked.

I explained that the local government authorities had informed me that it was illegal to conduct meetings in the open air and gather many people to speak to them. Two days earlier, I had met the president of our church in Kigali to ask him if he could negotiate the authorization. When I learned that it had been impossible for him to get the authorization, I had asked him to lend me his car and driver so I could try myself. I had just attempted to do so that day and failed. I had also asked different influential people in Kigali to help; they, too, had tried and failed.

"I was still praying about it before you came to see me," I said to Carl.

After I told him the reason for my discouragement, he offered to help.

"I know the mayor of Kigali City. She is a senior officer in the army, and we met during the genocide when I was trying to save the people." His words put a smile back on my face.

"Get ready. Tomorrow morning, I will come and pick you up. You and I will go to meet her. I believe she will help us!" Carl said with enthusiasm.

This was great! I thought I was dreaming. God was in control, and He would prove that when one moves to serve Him, things that appear to be hindrances are not hindrances at all! Mountains can be leveled, and seas may become dry land when Jesus is present!

The next morning, Carl and I went through the Seventh-day Adventist Union office before proceeding to see the mayor of the city. In this place, God would work another miracle. Right in the corridor of the church headquarters, I met a gentleman who called me by name, though we had never met before.

"Are you Phodidas?" he asked.

"Yes!" I replied.

"How is the youth program coming?" he inquired.

"It's all fine," I said. "We are busy making arrangements for several big meetings with the youth."

An American Refuses to Leave

"I believe you need some money for the meetings, don't you?" he asked.

"Yes, we do!" I responded in amazement.

"How much money do you need?" he asked further.

"Enough to purchase two hundred Bibles for the first meeting," I said.

"Anything else?" he inquired.

"We also need money to transport singers to the meetings," I told him.

He then asked me to give him a detailed list of all the things we needed and assured me that he would provide the money. As I discovered later, this gentleman was the director of the Church Ministries department based in our church headquarters in Abidjan, Ivory Coast. Later, I learned that Carl had talked to this man the night before and had informed him of our plans to conduct a massive preaching effort in Kigali and that we lacked sufficient funds for the project. God had answered our prayers and taken care of the financial obstacles.

Now there was still one problem, which was actually the main one. It was about 9:00 A.M. on Friday morning, the day before the meetings were to begin. We had informed all the churches in Kigali where to go the following Saturday. The people had invited many visitors. Choirs and churches were ready. But I still had no authorization. Only a few people knew about the problem we faced. These were praying and asking God to work a miracle.

From the union office, Carl and I went to see the mayor of Kigali City, but she was not available for us. Being a very busy person, Carl promised me he would go get his laptop computer and work from the reception area of the mayor's office while we waited for her to finish her meeting.

A few minutes later, he came back. This time he was on a motorcycle. He asked me to keep watch over it outside while he waited inside. An hour passed, then two, and at last close to three hours passed. Carl was working in his new office—the reception area of the mayor's office! I was still entreating God to act. I knew this was His work, and I was just playing my role as an instrument in His hands.

At sunset, I saw Carl coming out of the building. He was smiling, and I knew that we had received the authorization to hold the meetings. Our God had worked a great miracle! Carl handed me the official letter from the mayor.

Leaders who knew what I was going through were still waiting for me to come and inform them about the outcome of our visit to the mayor. They had asked their church members to wait after a vespers program for an important announcement. The people rejoiced and sang praises to the Lord as I came into the church that evening and read with full voice the authorization letter from the mayor.

The following day, Kigali was a hive of activity as cars, buses, and taxis streamed to the Muhima Seventh-day Adventist Church. Church members came from over twenty churches in and around Kigali. There were many Adventist youth groups in uniform who directed people to the places where we were holding the meetings.

It surprised the people of the city to see what was going on. One mission now united all the Seventh-day Adventists in this area, and they were modeling unity in the aftermath of the genocide. We conducted forty-two evangelistic efforts in Kigali in two months, during which we baptized about 640 people in the first baptism.

Following this city-wide program, we conducted several other evangelistic meetings in and outside of Kigali. Thousands gave their lives to Jesus, and the church of God once again felt enthusiasm for missions. We climbed mountains and went into valleys, reaching out to the unreached areas of Rwanda, such as Byumba, in the northern part of the country, where there were still traditional religions.

Today, with the efforts of the church leaders and lay members, the flame burns still brighter! Thousands and thousands are giving their lives to Jesus. The only problem—and this is true not just for Rwanda—is that we need to make sure the people we are converting to Jesus are not joining the church just to become Christians in name only! This is important when considering the work being done in Rwanda and elsewhere in the world.

People around the globe are being impressed by God concerning the impending judgment soon to come upon the entire world. In Rwanda, the most important evidence that God is ready to use His people, just as He did on the day of Pentecost, happened in 2016. It was during the Total Member Involvement (TMI) campaign in which the president of the world Seventh-day Adventist Church and almost all the church leaders took part. At the end of two weeks, in about two thousand sites, pastors baptized close to one hundred thousand people! After this TMI program, I also conducted three more evangelistic efforts which resulted in over five hundred people being baptized as soon as the meetings were over.

An American Refuses to Leave

I praise God that I have always been part of the organizing committees of the evangelistic efforts in Rwanda. Upon the request of my leaders, I have chaired several committees which resulted in positive evangelistic outcomes. Knowing the situation of the church in Rwanda and elsewhere in several other countries, I pray that we will do more than we have done.

There is a need now for more nurturing and discipleship training strategies. If not done, we have no assurance that those who are being converted today will be any different from the Rwandan Christian masses who became involved in the genocide against Tutsis, killing more than a million of their fellow believers.

Pray for my people, the Rwandans, and the church in Rwanda, so that peace and love will abound and prevail. Rwandans have gone through so much! I thank God because, even though what happened in Rwanda is beyond human understanding, what God has been doing now is also beyond our ability to comprehend. Please pray for the church of God in the world to do the work of preparing a people who will not succumb to temptation when the time of trial comes but will have the ability to stand firm and be faithful until the end.

God bless you!